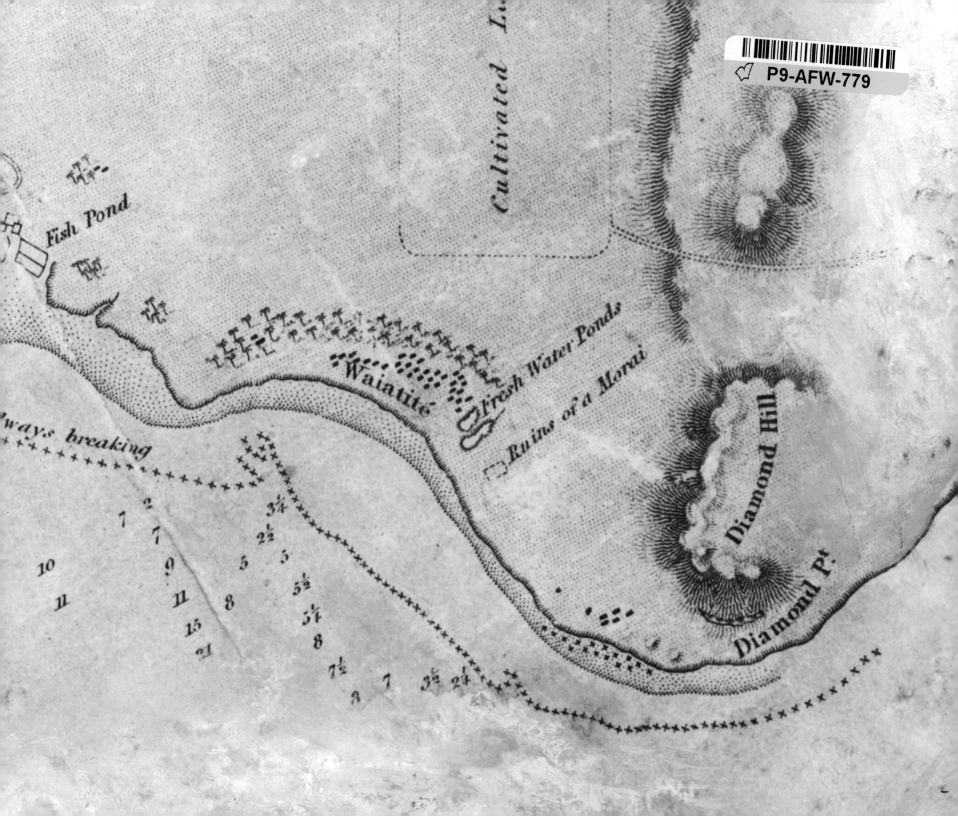

Fish Pond

Cultivated L...

Waiatiti

Fresh Water Ponds

Ruins of a Morai

Diamond Hill

Diamond P.t

...ways breaking

7

2

3¼

2½

10

7

9

5

5

5½

11

11

8

5¼

15

8

21

7½

7

3½

2¼

8

The View from Diamond Head

ROYAL RESIDENCE TO URBAN RESORT

O Waikīkī! O scene of peace!
O home of beauty and of dreams!
No haven in the isles of Greece
Can chord the harp to sweeter themes;
For houris *haunt the broad* lanais,
While scented zephyrs cool the lea,
And, looking down from sunset skies,
The angels smile on Waikīkī.

—Rollin M. Daggett

The View from Diamond Head

ROYAL RESIDENCE TO URBAN RESORT

by Don Hibbard and David Franzen

 AN EDITIONS LIMITED BOOK

Published by Editions Limited
        1123 Kapahulu Avenue
        Honolulu, Hawaii 96816

Produced by Gaylord H. Wilcox and David A. Rick

Marketing: Aaronetta Kandarian

Editor: Ruth Gurnani-Smith

Format design: Lester Yamamoto
Page design and layout: Ruth Gurnani-Smith/Kereru Arts
Mechanical art: Lisa Pongrace

First Printing November 1986
Second Printing January 1987

Titles and folios set in Garamond italic
Text set in 10/12 Palatino
Captions set in 10/11 Palatino

Library of Congress Cataloging-in-Publication Data

Hibbard, Don
    The View from Diamond Head

    Includes bibliography and index

    1. Land use—Hawai'i—Honolulu—History 2. Land use—Hawai'i—O'ahu—History 3.
Waikiki (Honolulu, Hawai'i)—History   I. Franzen, David, 1949-   II. Title HD268.H66H53
1986   333.77'13'0996931   86-19625   ISBN 0-915013-02-9

Printed in Japan

This book is dedicated to Moani
and our other offspring nestled within
the book and other intimate places.

Introduction & Acknowledgements

Standing on the summit of Diamond Head, 760 feet above sea level, one can survey the azure Pacific, rolling endlessly from the horizon to Hawai'i's shores. To the left an unobstructed panorama of Koko Head is offered, and to the rear stand the majestic Ko'olau mountains, the rim of a crater far greater than that of Diamond Head. But the view which demands the most attention is that to the right, where the city of Honolulu, and more immediately, Waikīkī, is laid out before the hiker. From here, atop Diamond Head, one can obtain an overview of Waikīkī.

This book is a series of vignettes, an album of impressions that also provides an overview of Waikīkī, an area geographically smaller than Honolulu Airport's reef runway, but an image far larger than all the Hawaiian islands combined. To understand the physical environment that mirrors the mythos of this miniscule strip of sand is the intention of this book. Our viewscreen attempts to focus on the meaning of this famous beach within our Island society, to answer the question: what is Waikīkī?

Such an answer transcends the district and concerns the State, for Waikīkī is a microcosm, a vision of what Hawai'i has gone through in the years since Statehood. It encapsulates not only our society's highest aspirations, but also its growing pains and concerns. It reflects our situation, but much more than that it discloses our dreams and ideals, and this is why we start the book with the past.

Dreams of the past linger in people's minds long after the psycho-physical manifestations that nurtured these apparitions have disappeared. Ghosts of yesterday are real and more often than not the glamour of these fleeting mirages define a place more vividly than its contemporary scene. For Waikīkī, the amorphous memory of a less crowded, supposedly simpler way of life refracts the light of today and lends a subliminal presence to the area.

The past also encompasses people's unfulfilled hopes for tomorrow. Waikīkī is not the same place for those residents who have witnessed and lived through the changes of the past thirty to seventy years, as it is for those who have seen it today for the first time. Recognition of the relationship between the present situation and its antecedents enhances the understanding of a place, and allows perceptions to travel beyond the surface.

By looking at what 'used to be' we better comprehend not only the extent of alteration but also adverse reactions of some local people to the current scene. For them Waikīkī is not Hawai'i. However, to understand the district of today, the book moves beyond the fact that Waikīkī is different, and examines the function of the area, and strives to define this urban resort in its own terms.

This book concentrates on Waikīkī's built environment because the physical setting is not only a response to a society's needs, but also a reflection of its values. More than offering shelter in a climate that requires very little, Island architecture, at its best, embodies the convictions of our people with regard to their sense of place. Just as the pyramids of Egypt or the cathedrals of France stand as statements of their culture, so too, Waikīkī's more outstanding buildings present images of our society and Hawai'i.

Looking at the built environment from this perspective, the chapter on Today does not directly address current urban issues such as traffic, overcrowding, crime, etc.. Instead it concentrates on the city of the mind, of feelings and imagination. It is this city that has made Waikīkī famous around the world, and it is in the light of these images that solutions to Waikīkī's concrete problems need to be formulated. A people-oriented space, Waikīkī remains clean and green, handling approximately four million mostly satisfied customers each year.

By considering the past and the built environment, *The View from Diamond Head* implicitly deals with change as observed in a specific place. Physical change comes in response to human needs and desires. For Waikīkī the needs and desires have been dramatic ones, and in the last two centuries the district has experienced at least five major transformations. With Western contact, the district moved from the mainstream to a backwash of activity. As the nineteenth century advanced, and people around the world made the ocean rather than the mountains their primary holiday destination, Waikīkī became an increasingly popular retreat and recreational area, and by the turn of the century it had attained renown as a world famous beach. This fame led to the destruction of the area's traditional, but incompatible, agricultural base, and the development of an increasingly resort-oriented, urban perspective. The latter eventually culminated in the high-rise skyline of today and a population density of 128 people per acre. As such the district well serves as a model for the changes that have transpired, or could still possibly happen, throughout the Islands.

A long, slow process brought this book together. Over the years, David and I have received invaluable assistance, advice, encouragement, words of wisdom, etc. from many people, a number of whom stand out. First and foremost our mahalo goes forth to Nathan Nāpōkā, who contributed much more than the opening essay. We greatly appreciated his informative and critical review of the manuscript, and support throughout the project. Nathan, thank you for an ear that could listen and an opinion worthy of respect.

Next we offer our mahalo to Barbara Mills at the Hawaiʻi Visitors Bureau for suggesting that a magazine proposal beset by difficulties, was too good not to be pursued as a book.

A debt of gratitude is owed to Gavan Daws, Francis Oda, Charles Sutton, and Jane Silverman who freely offered their thoughts on the subject, and to Don Bremner, Alan Gowans, Ron Lee, and Jim McCutcheon for not only their viewpoints, but also their perceptive comments on portions of the manuscript.

We also wish to thank the congenial and cooperative people employed by numerous repositories of historical information, who not only made the book a pleasure to research, but provided invaluable information, insights, and leads. These include the staff at the Hawaiʻi State Archives, especially Mary Ann Akao, Herb Arai, Kay Cho, Susan Shaner, Carol Silva, and Richard Thompson; Betty Kam and Clarice Chinen at the Bishop Museum; Charlie Okino and Kazutaka Saiki of the Hawaiʻi State Survey Division; Barbara Dunn at the Hawaiian Historical Society; Lela Goodell and Mary Jane Knight at the Hawaiian Mission Children's Society; Verna Miura and Kathleen Kudo at the City and County of Honolulu Municipal Reference Library; Proserfina Strona at the Hawaiʻi Public Library; John McLaughlin and Tom Fairfull at the U.S. Army Museum of Hawaii; and Warren Nishimoto and Michi Kodama-Nishimoto at the University of Hawaii Oral History Project.

A word of appreciation is also extended to all the merchants, resident managers and staff of the hotels, restaurants and condominiums whose *kokua* and positive feedback made the contemporary photographs possible.

Finally, we wish to thank Mrs. Joseph Gilman, Charles Uhlmann, Jack Gilmar, Dave Sox, Wayne Souza, Steve Sallis, Augie Salbosa, Jack Schweigert, Manya Vohrig, Mrs. Frank Midkiff, Keith and Dolly Steiner, Malcolm McLeod, Henry Inn, Nancy Bannick, Jessie Matthias, Peter Thacker, Father Yim, Betty Tartar, DeSoto Brown, Michailyn Chou, Aki Chun, Buck Buchwach, Bob King, Sophia Mumford, Muriel Flanders, and the numerous other people who filled informational voids, provided photographs, and made it all a bit more real.

Don J. Hibbard
Kāneʻohe, Hawaii

CONTENTS

YESTERDAY

Yesterday

The Seat of Power
by Nathan Nāpōkā

When old Hawaiians refer to Oʻahu they recall, *'ke one 'ai ali'i o Kākuhihewa'*, or the chief-consuming sands of Kākuhihewa. Kākuhihewa was a famous *ali'i* (chief) who ruled Oʻahu during the late 1500s. He lived at Ulukou, Waikīkī on the spot now occupied by the Moana Hotel. His reign was marked by great prosperity during which all the invading chiefs from other islands were defeated. The sands at Ulukou were known as the chief-eating sands because of the strength of this great chief. Kākuhihewa's Waikīkī came to epitomize the golden era of aboriginal Hawaiian history and is mentioned frequently in traditional Hawaiian chant as well as contemporary song.

Five generations before Kākuhihewa's birth, circa 1450, Māʻilikūkāhi first established Waikīkī as the government center for the island of Oʻahu. From this time until 1809, when Kamehameha I moved his court to Honolulu, Waikīkī was the seat of power for Oʻahu.

Originally Waikīkī encompassed a larger area than the section we are familiar with today. According to early survey descriptions the *ahupua'a* [land division] of Waikīkī was bounded by Honolulu on one side and Maunalua Bay on the other side, and included the valleys of Mānoa and Pālolo. The large *moku* [district] of Kona consisted of six *ahupua'a*, Waikīkī being one of them.

To the early Hawaiians Waikīkī offered a fine reef-protected beach that sufficiently accommodated their canoes. A deeper harbor was not needed until larger Western ships frequented the Islands—the situation which motivated Kamehameha I to move his court from Waikīkī to Honolulu.

Waikīkī was most significantly a rich taro producing area. From the time of Kalamakua, who lived in the first half of the fifteenth century, large *loko* [fishponds] dotted the landscape which was covered with taro *lo'i* [terraces]. Kalamakua is credited with starting the elaborate irrigation systems that survived until the beginning of the twentieth century. The springs that fed these taro lands were responsible for the name Waikīkī which literally means spouting waters.

The focal centers of chiefly culture in Waikīkī were the areas known as Helumoa and Ulukou or Kou, where the Royal Hawaiian and the Moana Hotels stand today. The ʻĀpuakēhau Stream emptied into the ocean midway between these two areas and at its mouth was the famous surfing spot called Kalehuawehe. From legendary times this area was the celebrated residence of high-ranking chiefs.

An uncle of John Papa ʻĪʻī, a noted Hawaiian scholar, was an attendant in the court of Kamehameha I whose residence was at Puaʻaliʻiliʻi, an area in Waikīkī which included all of Helumoa and ʻĀpuakēhau. At the age of 10 ʻĪʻī moved in with his uncle

View of Waititi and

at Kawehewehe, the land adjacent to Helumoa. According to him, the King had built a stone house at Pua'ali'ili'i and his favorite wife, Ka'ahumanu and her retainers went there to 'while away the time'.

While the *ali'i* engaged in leisurely pursuits the *maka'āinana* [commoners] provided the labor and, in turn, the food for everyone's daily existence. They tended the elaborate agricultural field system as well as engaged in daily fishing activities. Harriet Newell Foster Deming observed a typical ocean harvest on Waikīkī Beach in the 1850s:

> *The event of each morning was to watch the return of the fishing canoes with their daily catch. Native women and children from round about came to help in the division of the fish. According to the unwritten law one fish in every five belonged to the King. Sometimes four canoes would be drawn up on the beach at once, filled with shining beauties in nets . . . the wealth of color fascinated us as we hung over the sides of the canoes watching the bronzed fishermen who, naked except for a loincloth, scooped up the fish in their hands and laid them in piles on the sand. The head of every fifth fish was bitten off to count it for the King.*

This diet of fish was supplemented with *poi* pounded from the taro corm. These two foods were the staples of Hawaiian existence. Mrs. Deming also had special comments to make on the preparation of *poi*:

> *The natives in the spring house as we call it invited us to join them in eating poi, which they made every few days, but after watching the process we were not very eager. The big kanaka who fathered the family sat cross-legged on the ground pounding taro with a stone pestle until the sweat rolled off his half naked body and into the sticky mass, while the women looked on, laughing and chatting, as they mixed the taro pulp with water and kneaded it with their hands in large wooden bowls. To really enjoy poi, one does not want to see it made.*

Up until Kamehameha I's reign, Waikīkī thrived as a Hawaiian community. Not until the end of his rule do we see the center of control shift across the plains to Honolulu Harbor. *Kāhuna* [priests] performed formal rituals for the ruling aristocracy

Waikīkī in 1825, as drawn by Robert Dampier, who came to Hawai'i on the H.M.S. Blonde, the ship that returned the remains of Kamehameha II and his wife after the monarchs' untimely deaths in England.

Diamond Head and the royal Helumoa coconut grove in the 1870s. At one time this grove consisted of nearly 10,000 trees. According to legend the first tree was planted during the reign of Kākuhihewa. The phantom rooster of Pālolo, Kaʻauhelemoa, appeared before the chief scratching the earth. On that spot, the chief ordered a coconut planted. The resulting grove was called Helumoa.

The royal coconut grove at Helumoa during the 1880s, as seen from the bank of ʻĀpuakēhau Stream. Remnants of the grove still stand in the east courtyard of the Royal Hawaiian hotel.

The four wizard stones of Ulukou are the tangible remnants of Kapaemahu, Kahaloa, Kapuni and Kinohi, soothsayers from Kahiki [Tahiti] who settled on this spot prior to 1400 A.D. They were unsexed by nature and their skill in the healing arts made them famous all over Oʻahu. As a reminder of their life in Hawaiʻi, thousands of people carried the four monumental tablets nearly two miles from Kaimukī to this place. A young chiefess was sacrificed during the consecration of the stones when the wizards transferred their powers into them. With the conclusion of this ceremony the wizards vanished, never to be seen again.

during the height of activity in Waikīkī and thus many *heiau* [temples] were constructed here. A famous *heiau* was built at Helumoa where the Maui chief Kauhiakama was sacrificed in 1610 by Oʻahu chief Kaʻihikapu after an unsuccessful invasion of Oʻahu.

Seven other major *heiau* also stood in Waikīkī, according to Thrum. Kamehameha I was the last *aliʻi* to use them in the formal practice of traditional Hawaiian religion. In Waikīkī he used Papaʻenaʻena *heiau*, the present site of the Hawaiʻi School for Girls, to offer sacrifices to the Hawaiian gods.

One of these sacrifices in Waikīkī during the great pestilence of 1804 was excruciatingly described by Tyerman and Bennett:

During the plague the King repaired to the great marae (heiau) at Wytiti to conciliate the god whom he supposed to be angry. The priests recommended a ten day's tabu, the sacrifice of three human victims, four hundred hogs, as many coconuts, and an equal number of branches of plantains. Three men, who had been guilty of the enormous turpitude of eating coconuts with the old Queen (the present King's mother) were

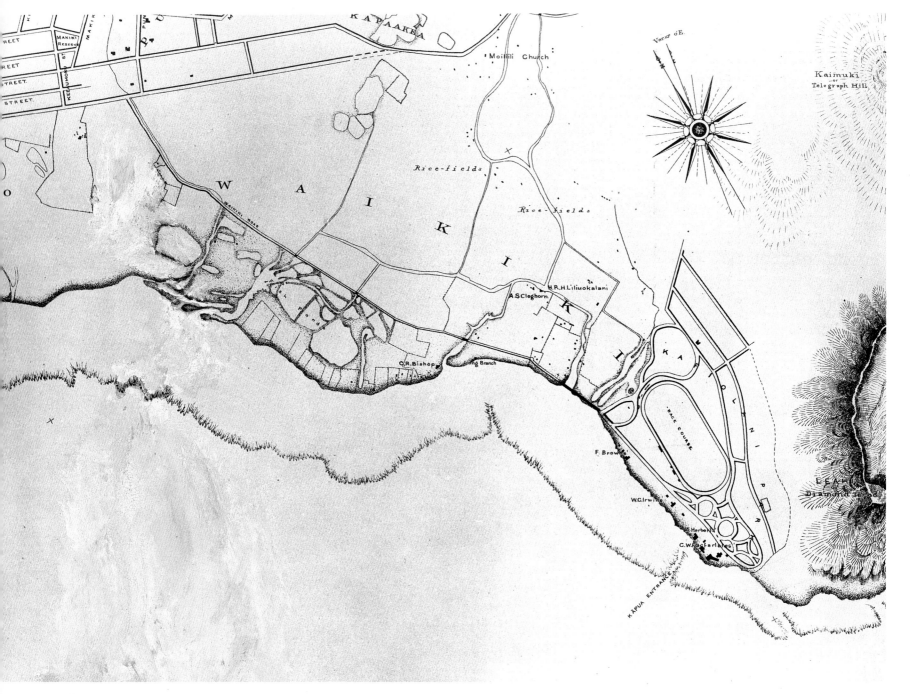

Map of Waikīkī drawn by S.E. Bishop in 1888.

accordingly seized and led to the marae. But there being yet three days before the offerings could be duly presented, the eyes of the victims were scooped out, the bones of their arms and legs were broken, and they were deposited in a house, to await the coup de grace on the day of sacrifice. While these maimed and miserable creatures were in the height of their suffering, some persons, moved by curiosity, visited them in prison, and found them neither raving nor desponding, but sullenly singing the national hula, as though they were insensible of the past, and indifferent to the future. When the slaughtering time arrived, one of them was placed under the legs of the idol, and the other two were laid with the hogs and fruit upon the altar frame. They were then beaten with clubs upon the shoulders till they died of blows. This was told us by an eyewitness of the murderous spectacle.

This was one of the last sacrifices offered in Waikīkī under the traditional Hawaiian religious ceremonies. The old system of taboos was overthrown by Kamehameha I's son immediately after the ruler's death in 1819.

Although the slopes of Diamond Head have stood witness to some of the bloodiest rituals of Hawaiian religion, this same mountain has been the enchanting landmark that lingers on as the symbol of Waikīkī. From earliest times people have been attached to the curving white sand beaches with the many shades of blue water, punctuated by Diamond Head in the distance.

The legendary figure Kawelo came to Waikīkī during Kākuhihewa's reign to participate in surfing and wrestling matches at the Helumoa coconut grove, which still stands on the Royal Hawaiian Hotel grounds today. When he departed from Waikīkī to return to his homeland of Kaua'i, he chanted a love song for Kou, his sweetheart at Waikīkī and the name of the lands where Kākuhihewa resided:

Aloha Kou e, Aloha Kou,	Farewell to thee, farewell Kou,
Ke aloha mai nei Kou ia'u,	The love of Kou is within me,
Ka hoa hele i ka makani,	My companion of the windy days
I ka 'āpa'apa'a anu o Ahulu nei.	And the cold of Ahulu.
E ualo mai ana ia'u nā niu o Pai,	The coconut trees of Pai are calling me back,
E 'ena'ena mai ana i ku'u maka,	They appear as raging fire to my eyes,
Ke 'd'ā o Kuamānu'unu'u,	Like the volcanic rocks at Kuamānu'unu'u
'I'iau e ki'i, e kui, a lei—e,	I am tempted to get them, to string them, and to wear them,
Nā 'ākulikuli papa o Huia nei la,	The 'ākulikuli blossoms there at Huia
E ualo mai ana ia'u—e.	For they are calling me back there.

The love of Kawelo for Kou symbolizes the romantic obsession with Waikīkī that has lasted through the centuries. Although the place names in the song have been lost in antiquity, the emotions associated with them are still with us today.

View of Diamond Head from Honolulu, by G.H. Burgess, 1857.

Victorian Waikīkī—The Playground of Royalty

by Marilyn Stassen-McLaughlin

Queen Lili'uokalani's cottage at Hamohamo, circa 1880. The lands at Hamohamo were given to the future Queen by her mother Ana Keohokālole in 1859.

During the 1820s and 1830s the Christian church and the whaling industry discovered Hawai'i, bringing numerous foreigners to the Islands' shores. Correspondingly, the native Hawaiian population rapidly dwindled. These factors, coupled with Kamehameha I's shifting his headquarters to Honolulu Harbor, marked an end to Waikīkī as both an agricultural center and the seat of power for O'ahu. Many of the district's taro *lo'i* were abandoned, and by 1852 King Kamehameha I's coral residence at Waikīkī was "falling into rapid decay". The *heiau* the king once used now appeared to visitors as vestiges of some ancient time, and in 1866 Mark Twain referred to the district as "historic Waikīkī".

Waikīkī maintained an informal style of life, and as Honolulu grew and became more sophisticated, this sandy shore became a retreat for the *ali'i*. As the only place

William C. Lunalilo's Waikīkī residence at Kaluaokau, which the King willed to Queen Emma upon his death in 1874. The dowager Queen had Papa'ena'ena heiau dismantled to use its rocks to build a wall around this estate.

The Bishop residence at Helumoa, circa 1880.

King Kamehameha V's cottage at Helumoa, built in 1866. The King purchased this ocean front property in 1865 from Charles Guillou, and three years later, in 1868, bought from Kaʻōpua and Nāhua, descendants of Kaleiheana, the neighboring lands of Helumoa.

close to the city with a beach and inviting waters, Waikīkī was the obvious locale for visitors and members of Hawaiʻi's upper class to go in search of relaxation and recreation. Here one could lie back, enjoy the soothing balm of the sun and ocean, and escape the more proper ways of Honolulu.

Kamehameha IV, Kamehameha V, and Lunalilo, who consecutively ruled Hawaiʻi from 1854 to 1874, all had residences in the area. These were typically unpretentious wooden structures, some with grass roofs, but as the century moved into its last quarter more fashionable homes and modern conveniences were added to the royal beach cottages. Princess Bernice Pauahi Bishop and her husband remodeled the thatched roof cottage of Kamehameha V, making "it into a large residence and added accessory buildings where cooking was done." Similarly, Archibald Cleghorn built his large Victorian house next door to the simple bungalow, the childhood home of his daughter Princess Kaʻiulani. Their estate, ʻĀinahau, consisted of ten acres laid out in

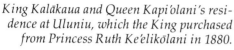

King Kalākaua and Queen Kapi'olani's residence at Uluniu, which the King purchased from Princess Ruth Ke'elikōlani in 1880.

gardens, winding walks, artificial lakes, and groves of coconut palms. Mr. Cleghorn also did much of the landscape design work for Kawaiahao Church, Thomas Square, and Kapi'olani Park.

The large home and beautiful gardens at 'Āinahau were a showplace for Ka'iulani, the heir apparent to the Hawaiian throne. The new house was a "white frame structure of two storeys, with wings at either end and a wide verandah extending across the front. . . . Much was made of the screens, so universal in the United States, but strangely enough not in ordinary use in that mosquito-ridden land." Peacocks, so loved by Ka'iulani, roamed freely on this estate and the nearby estates of Uluniu and Pualeilani, home sites of Kalākaua and Kapi'olani. Hawaiians called Ka'iulani the 'Princess of Peacocks', and because she loved Chinese jasmine, they named the flower *pīkake*, their word for peacock.

With its improved housing, Waikīkī began to be a center for social gatherings. At parties Mrs. Bishop encouraged guests to remain after dinner and play charades, and she would send her retainers about the neighborhood asking friends to join in informal gatherings. Cakes, jellies, and lemonade were served. If the moon were bright, horseback rides might be organized or better yet, rides on King Kalākaua's boat, which one guest described, "Aboard the boat Mrs. Bishop, Lili'uokalani, and the other ali'i [sang] . . . accompanied by guitars, we rowed the harbor."

In comparison to Waikīkī, Honolulu was frequently abuzz with more formal calling days and regal receptions. At the center of this bustling social life was King Kalākaua, who had visited and come away impressed with Queen Victoria's court. Many Honolulu visitors rode in carriages to 'Iolani Palace, danced at elegant balls, and ate

11

Archibald Scott Cleghorn of 'Āinahau

'Āinahau, the home architect Clinton B. Ripley designed for Archibald Cleghorn circa 1890. 'Āinahau means cold land, and derives from the cool Mānoa breeze which kept this area cooler than other parts of Waikī-kī. This fine residence burned to the ground in 1921.

A wealthy merchant and man about town, Archibald Cleghorn, at the age of thirty-seven married Miriam Likelike, the nineteen-year-old great-granddaughter of chief Kepo'okalani, a cousin of King Kamehameha I. This marriage, on 20 September 1870, brought the Scotsman into the midst of Hawaiian royalty and governmental affairs when his wife's brother, David Kalākaua, became king in 1874. The King appointed Cleghorn to the House of Nobles and upon the death of John Dominis in 1891, Queen Lili'uokalani made him governor of O'ahu.

One of the more prominent men of his day, Cleghorn played an instrumental role in the founding of Kapi'olani Park in 1877. He served as vice-president, and later president of the Kapi'olani Park Association, and planned the landscaping of the park. The stately ironwood trees that adorn Kalākaua Avenue's route through the park were planted under his supervision, as were the grand banyans at Thomas Square.

Cleghorn not only beautified Waikīkī through his work at Kapi'olani Park, but also at his estate, 'Āinahau, which he had purchased in 1872 for $300. Inheriting a love of horticulture from his father, Cleghorn lavishly landscaped this parcel, making it "the most beautiful private estate in the Hawaiian Islands". At first he used it as a country retreat. However, it soon became his family's primary residence, and his stately home on Emma Street was turned over to the Pacific Club, an organization he had joined in 1853 and presided over for forty-six years. As a royal residence in Waikīkī, 'Āinahau was the scene of various parties and entertainments, and visitors such as Robert Louis

Cleghorn at 'Āinahau with his family.
Princess Ka'iulani is seated to his left.

Governor
Archibald
Scott
Cleghorn

Stevenson departed the Islands with fond memories of the estate. Not only a site of pleasant pastimes, these lands also were associated with grief and tragedy. Here, Princess Likelike died on 2 February 1887, at the age of thirty-six, and twelve years later, in 1899, Cleghorn's daughter, Ka'iulani, passed away here in the springtime of her life, at the age of twenty-four. Following her death Cleghorn led a less active life, although he remained involved in the affairs of Queens Hospital, and in 1909 he became its first elected president, a post which previously had been occupied by either the reigning monarch or the territorial governor.

Cleghorn died of heart failure at 'Āinahau on 1 November 1910. Several months before his death he had witnessed the reinterment of Likelike and Ka'iulani into crypts in the Royal Mausoleum. This event left him "strangely agitated", and some speculated it led to his own demise. His remains were accorded every official honor of the Territory, and as a drizzling rain drifted down Nu'uanu from the Pali, his casket was placed in a crypt next to those of his wife and daughter. The *Pacific Commercial Advertiser* editorally described him as, "A gentleman of the old school, one who regretted the passing away of the monarchy, but who accepted the new condition time brought to the Islands and lent his aid in helping shape events for the best."

Cleghorn's will left 'Āinahau to the Territory of Hawai'i, with the stipulation that it become Kai'ulani Park. Both the 1911 and 1913 legislatures refused this gift, thanks to the efforts of Representative Archibald S. Robertson, one of the heirs that inherited the land after the park offer was rejected. The estate was eventually subdivided and sold for residential purposes, which the *Pacific Commercial Advertiser* found to be "a severe shock to the sentiments".

sumptuous meals. The ladies dressed in high fashion gowns not unlike those of their royal hostesses. This display of courtly extravagance reflected Kalākaua's desire to create a Hawaiian Victorian society. A British visitor pronounced Honolulu, "too glary", but most people were impressed with the palatial show.

However, as much as Kalākaua and other *ali'i* of that period enjoyed the town social whirl, they would frequently retire to Waikīkī's shores, greet their old friends, relax, and perhaps keep in touch with the ocean, the sunsets and the solitude. Just as Lunalilo earlier visited his Waikīkī residence, and enjoyed "the quiet life of Waikīkī and living simply on fish and poi with his native friends"; so too, Princess Lili'uokalani, surrounded by the formalities of town society and her royal responsibilities, looked forward to retreats to her Waikīkī residence. She wrote in her diary in 1885: (7 February) "Went out to Waikīkī ... very little was done." (11 February) "Spent the day in sleeping and eating at my bathing place ..." (20 February) "Went out to Waikīkī as usual ... did not do much ... my old friends came to see me ...". When added duties were pressed upon the Princess, she slipped out to her beach retreat early in the morning: (2 April) "Went to Waikīkī about 6:00 AM to fish. Went to Bishop's fishing ground got lots of Ohios [sic]. Got home at half past twelve, had lunch, a soup, then dressed for my reception at 3:00." Quite a schedule! Perhaps the happy morning in Waikīkī contributed to the easy grace with which Lili'uokalani hosted the royal receptions, so admired by English and American visitors.

Princess Lydia (Lili'uokalani) liked receiving friends at her Waikīkī residence. One party in the late nineteenth century lasted from 11:00 AM until sunset. The *lū'au* setting featured ancient hulas and chants plus games "displaying Hawaiian athletic prowess". The hula was featured at many of Queen Lili'uokalani's parties including one given at her home on Kūhiō Beach. This birthday party was limited to fifty people since the house and grounds were not spacious enough to accommodate more. The Queen stopped the dancers upon the arrival of the first American Bishop of St. Andrew's Cathedral, Henry Bond Restarick, and his wife. The Queen thought the Bishop would be offended by the hula. Surprisingly he asked, "Why did the girls stop their dance? I was enjoying it immensely".

A popular spot for informal evenings was King Kalākaua's boat house in Waikīkī. Nelly Strickland, a journalist who visited in 1890, reported that, "The Boat House is a light, pretty structure decorated gayly interiorly and with an excellent floor for dancing. ... After we had feasted and danced chairs were placed, and the guests, about fifty in number, witnessed the native dance called 'The Hoolah' ... [which] must be seen ... It is a swaying of the body, arms, hands, and head to a slow weird rhythmic song."

Hawaiian royalty enjoyed entertaining guests, and their homes were centers for *lū'au* and their accompanying native entertainment. On these occasions people were served "everything that can be roasted or fried until almost comatose", then they were "revived with ice cream". Other parties included more formal meals with Victorian amusements such as parlor games and croquet. For all parties the beach itself provided surfing, outrigger canoe rides, and romps in the ocean.

Map of Waikīkī drawn by M.D. Monsarrat, 10 July 1897. The map notes the land ownership for each parcel, and also includes the location of the various royal residences in the district.

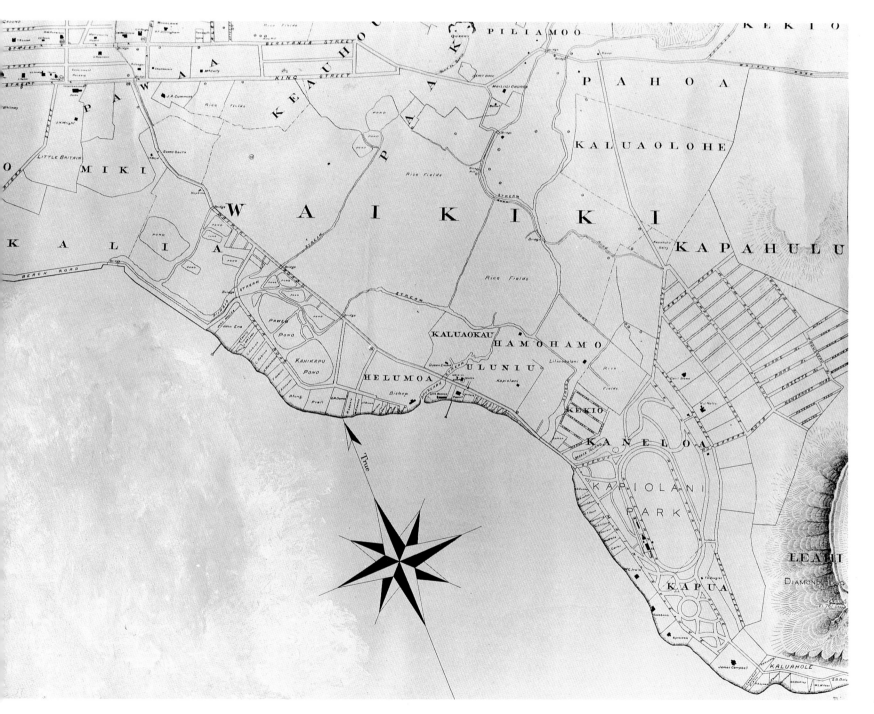

15

Croquet players at ʻĀinahau. Princess Kaʻiulani is to the right, and her half-sister Anne sits in front.

The arrival in Honolulu of the Duke of Edinburgh, Prince Alfred Ernest Albert, the second son of Queen Victoria, in July 1869, was perhaps the social event of nineteenth century Hawaii. As the first member of a European royal family to visit the Islands, the Duke was regally received. During his ten day stay, he attended a number of receptions and dinners, including a lūʻau hosted by Mrs. John Dominis (the future Queen Liliʻuokalani). Held at Hamohamo on 27 July 1869, the lūʻau was intended to be a strictly Hawaiian affair, with the Duke, his cadre of officers, and foreign consuls being the only foreigners invited. The King, the dowager Queens Kalama and Emma, Mrs. Bernice Pauahi Bishop, Princess Ruth Keʻelikōlani, Miriam Likelike, and numerous others attended the celebration, which ran from noon until five in the afternoon when a storm ended the festivities. The Hawaiian Gazette described the lūʻau as "the largest feast that has been spread, for many years," and noted that, "every variety of Hawaiian food was offered, to the amusement of the distinguished guest." The Pacific Commercial Advertiser staidly reported a more missionary perspective: "We regret to have to chronicle the fact that the disgraceful Hula-dance was a part of the programme, and trust for the sake of common decency that it may be the last time that this relic of heathenism may be performed before such an audience."

Not only did the kings, queens and their guests seek out Waikīkī, but independent travelers were urged to make the trip. Waikīkī of the late nineteenth century was considered "country". Imagine hiring a hack and paying twenty-five cents for each of the three miles to the shore or paying double fare on the mule drawn tram cars! Some visitors hired horses from the Pantheon Stable in downtown Honolulu and rode to the beach. Mr. Burton Holmes, a seasoned traveler, advised visitors to bring letters of introduction to "people of wealth or position" so that the newcomers could enjoy a lū'au in a "typical Honolulu house in Waikīkī, a charming suburb about three miles from the center of Honolulu."

On the other hand, monarchs were often honored guests at social events given by *haole* [Caucasians] who lived in Waikīkī. At one party he attended, Mr. Holmes said the host and hostess met him with *lei* "before he could reach the house". "Quaint Japanese maids in native costume" brought them appetizers and then he went to the lānai where the *lū'au* was spread. Ferns were laid on the floor. Stacked in the center and spilling out to the edges were pineapple, watermelon, other fruits, and sometimes a stalk of sugar cane. Everything was placed on the table at once—pink crabs, baby lobsters, baked mullet in tī leaves unwrapped by the hostess who broke it and passed around pieces to guests. The highest compliment was to "suck one's fingers as audibly as possible" and withdraw the fingers from the mouth with a "satisfied smack" in appreciation of the cuisine.

This audible smacking may have puzzled visitors who had been received primly to a high Victorian tea at the palace that very afternoon. Of course, some Waikīkī hostesses preferred more formal dinners and social gatherings, including lawn parties.

Ladies at 'Āinahau sometimes would play croquet at night. Each player would make her way with a "blazing torch in one hand grasping the mallet with the other," reported Maude Jones. During evening croquet games, ladies dressed in the latest fashion would often slosh through the wet grass, dirtying their white muslin dust catchers. Una Hunt Drage, one of the more liberated visitors to Honolulu, wrote that she felt "hoydenish, cracking away barehanded at the ball when others kept on their long white kid gloves which split." The character of Waikīkī encouraged such informality, and these Hawaiian ways, when placed in juxtapositon with Victorian culture, made Waikīkī particularly attractive to many nineteenth century visitors who appreciated the security of their proper *haole* culture but could also return to the United States or Europe and boast of adventures with the "noble savages".

Nowhere was this more apparent than in swimming in the ocean. Waikīkī bathing varied drastically from New England bathing. One visitor contrasted Nantucket/Newport "bathing" with its "half-hearted dips" to Waikīkī, where bathers "swim in every imaginable way . . . float, tread water, dive, plunge".

This bathing was done not only during the daytime. Drage reported on the freedom of nighttime beach activities as well. "The week of the full moon everyone bathes by moonlight, . . . Big waves swept me high in the air and then dropped me down into the trough, making the moon and stars stagger tipsily as if they and not I were being tossed about." Certainly this was a new experience for visiting bathing beauties who, covered from neck to ankle, gingerly ventured a toe into the ocean.

A royal lū'au given by King Kalākaua for Robert Louis Stevenson on 3 February 1889. Stevenson and his mother sit at the head of the spread with the King and his sister, the future Queen Lili'uokalani.

A royal lū'au given by King Kalākaua at his boathouse in the 1880s for the Hoffnungs.

18

Even Princess Ka'iulani, fresh from her stringent schooling in England, wrote to Lili'uokalani in 1893 about her delight with bathing: "About ten days ago Stella Lockett, Helen Parker and I went over to your place [at Waikīkī] and took a bath. The water was perfectly lovely. I have had only one dip in the sea so far. As my bathing suits have not arrived yet—we went in by moonlight in night gowns, when no one was around."

Princess Ka'iulani, like others, enjoyed moonlight swims, for the Waikīkī waters loosened some of the Victorian regulations that had been tightly plaited into the life of Hawaiian monarchs, *haole* residents and visitors alike.

Queen Lili'uokalani's pier at Ke'alohilani, now a part of Kūhiō Beach.

From Mosquitoes to Mansions

The lānai of the McInerny cottage, circa 1910. Now the location of the Kaimana Beach Hotel, the hau tree with its sheltering bowers still stands, although the Sans Souci pier, which is in the background, disappeared as a result of the 1982 Hurricane 'Iwa.

The casual tranquility of Waikīkī appealed not only to the *ali'i* who frequented the district, but also to a growing number of foreigners who lived in Hawai'i. The beach beckoned to these recent arrivals, and with the overthrow of the traditional land tenure system due to the Great Māhele of 1848 and the passage of legislation in 1850 which gave aliens the right to purchase land, new faces began to appear in Waikīkī.

The Kings, Queens and other native Hawaiian residents of the area soon found new neighbors in their midst—the Hillebrands, Montgomerys, and McLeans, to name but a few. Waikīkī soon took on a different character, "becoming a considerable place of resort", which Honolulu's merchants frequented "as a bathing place in the summer", or so reported Prince Lot Kamehameha to the 1860 Legislature.

Oceanfront view of the McInerny cottage, circa 1910. The trappings of mainland lifestyle were well evident in Waikīkī.

The government further facilitated the growth of the district when it expanded the ancient trail to Waikīkī into a road in the early 1860s. Thus by 1865 the *Pacific Commercial Advertiser* could note, "quite a little community of foreign families are now residing at the beach at Waikīkī," and in 1873 British visitor William R. Bliss could describe the area as, "a hamlet of plain cottages, stretching along the seashore, in the edge of cocoanut palms, whither the white people of Honolulu go to revel in bathing-clothes, mosquitoes and solitude."

Far-flung from the outer limits of civilization, sitting at least a full three miles from downtown, the denizens of this emerging suburban village had their share of hardships. The location of fresh water springs was not known to these refugees from the city, and in the early years they had to bring this precious commodity with them. This situation improved as the new gentry established a rapport, frequently through their servants, with the older residents of the community who pointed out and shared their water sources.

A more difficult problem to cope with were the mosquitoes, which had been

The beach in front of the Alfred Mitchell house in 1886. The substantial residence in the background belonged to William Irwin and is where the War Memorial Natatorium now stands.

introduced accidently to the Islands in 1826. Waikīkī's extensive ponds proved to be excellent breeding grounds, and many a visitor commented on the irritating presence of the *makika*, including Mark Twain, who in 1866, wrote, "There are a good many mosquitoes around tonight and they are rather troublesome; but it is a source of unalloyed satisfaction to me to know that the two millions I sat down on a minute ago will never sing again." The mosquitoes did not abandon their salubrious waters at Waikīkī until the 1920s when the Ala Wai Canal effectively drained the area.

Despite such difficulties, the lure of Waikīkī was undeniable. Throughout the last half of the nineteenth century, and on into the twentieth, people went there to enjoy its "surf bathing" and its quiet "change of atmosphere". The same charms that had impassioned Kawelo continued to exert their power, and as visitor George Leonard Chaney pointed out, the "seaside felicity" of Waikīkī seemed to offer "a promise of rest in its motionless life, and a chance for self-recovery in its self-forgetful solitude."

The dwellings built in mid-nineteenth century Waikīkī were modest affairs, simple cottages that served more as country retreats than as principle places of residence. It

Waikīkī Road, the main artery linking Waikīkī with downtown. The 1905 Territorial Legislature changed the name of this major thoroughfare to Kalākaua Avenue to commemorate the name of the former monarch "during whose reign Hawai'i made great advancement in material prosperity".

The Hawai'i Tramway's mule-drawn cars plied this highway from 1889 to 1903, when the Honolulu Rapid Transit's electric cars replaced them.

Waikīkī, circa 1880.

Cordelia Gilman sitting on Jacob Brown's lānai on a balmy day, circa 1908. This covered lānai was built on the beach which now fronts on the Halekūlani.

The Henry Bertelmann residence, built in the late 1880s near the base of Diamond Head. The counterrevolution of 1895 started at this peaceful cottage.

'On the Road to Waikīkī'. The bicycle was a mode of transportation very much in vogue in the pre-automobile years of the late 1890s.

Fisherman at Waikīkī during the 1890s.

The McInerny beach cottage, circa 1910. The McInernys purchased this property in 1903.

Sanford B. Dole's beach cottage at Kaluahole, the extreme tip of Diamond Head, circa 1905.

was not until the 1890s that larger houses appeared, including those of James Campbell, Frank Hustace and W.C. Peacock. Sporting turrets and/or gingerbread, these homes consciously followed the architectural fancies of their day. They delighted the eye and contributed an element of substantiality to the area. However, although commanding in size, these residences were soon dwarfed by the even more

The Frank Hustace residence, circa 1913. Built during the late 1890s, this rambling house stood adjacent to the Moana Hotel. In 1916 the hotel leased it as an employee's annex. In 1919 the Moana exercised its option to buy the house, which remained under the hotel's control until 1950 when it was razed to make way for the Surfrider Hotel.

The James Campbell residence, circa 1910. Located at the base of Diamond Head, near the intersection of Kalākaua Avenue and Diamond Head Road, James Campbell had this house built in the 1890s. Colonel Parker, the grandson of J.P. Parker, the founder of Parker Ranch on the island of Hawai'i, married Campbell's widow and later lived here. In the early 1920s the house was moved by barge to Punalu'u, where it stands today.

The William G. Irwin residence. Architect C.W. Dickey designed this stately mansion in 1899 for sugar industry magnate William G. Irwin. One of the earliest Spanish Mission Revival style houses in Hawai'i, it featured a verandah which wrapped completely around the house and opened onto large airy rooms. Although considered "an ideal Waikīkī residence" by the Pacific Commercial Advertiser it stood less than twenty-five years, as it became the site of the War Memorial Natatorium.

magnificent mansions erected at the turn of the century for James B. Castle, William G. Irwin, James Steiner and others. The presence of such fine homes gave Waikīkī a new air, "transforming this section of the city's suburbs from its former temporary summer residence character to one of luxuriant permanency."

The James Steiner residence. Built in 1912, this colonial style house followed plans drawn by Honolulu architects Ripley & Reynolds. With its round-the-corner lānai fronting on Kalākaua Avenue and rear lānai overlooking the beach, it remained a familiar Waikīkī landmark until demolished in 1950 as part of the Kūhio Beach improvement project. This gracious house had extremely open interior living spaces.

31

James B. Castle (bearded) and his guests sitting on the front lawn of his Waikīkī residence, Kainalu, circa 1902. By far the most grandiose house in Waikīkī, if not all of Honolulu, James B. Castle had this stunning residence built in 1899, on the site of the former Park Beach Hotel.

The Castle residence was designed by Oliver G. Traphagen, the architect of the Moana Hotel. This incredibly large and ultra impressive colonial style residence rivaled the hotel in its majesty and opulence. With its lānai overlooking the ocean on each of the three stories, it epitomized the luxury surrounding a number of the people deeply involved in Hawai'i's sugar industry at the turn of the century.

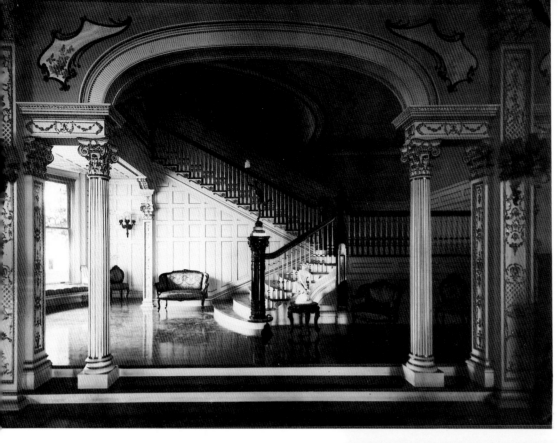

Entry hall, Kainalu

Castle died on 4 April 1918, and two years later the Benevolent Protective Order of the Elks purchased his Waikīkī residence for use as their club. Kainalu served in this capacity until 1959 when it was demolished. The present modest Elks Club was built in its stead.

The stained glass windows illuminating the stairway were specially ordered from the Tiffany Studios in New York. The only other two Tiffany windows in Hawai'i were commissioned by churches.

Castle had very close links with the prosperous sugar industry. The son of Samuel N. Castle, the founder of Castle & Cooke, he contributed heavily to the starting of the Ko'olau, Kahuku, and 'Ewa Sugar Plantations, and was instrumental in Alexander & Baldwins' eventual purchase of Claus Spreckels' Hawaiian Commerce and Sugar Company. He also was responsible for the construction of the Ko'olau Railroad and his financial backing made possible the Honolulu Rapid Transit System.

Main room, Kainalu

Living room, Deering residence.

C.W. Case Deering, who made his fortune in the manufacture of farm implements, commissioned Chicago architects Holabird and Roche to design this oceanfront residence in 1916. Chris Holmes, whose wealth derived from Fleishmann Yeast, purchased the house in 1933, for $76,000. During World War II Franklin D. Roosevelt stayed here. He secretly flew into Hawai'i to confer with Admiral Nimitz and General MacArthur concerning the United States' strategy in the Pacific: discussions that later resulted in the decision to invade the Philippine Islands rather than Formosa and China, thus allowing MacArthur to fulfill his prophetic, "I shall return". After World War II it was converted into the Queen's Surf restaurant and bar, which remained a famous night spot in Waikīkī until the house was demolished in 1971 as part of a beach improvement project.

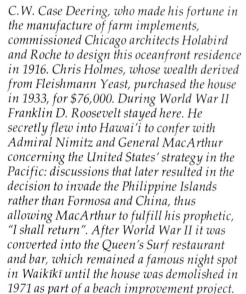

Second story lanai, Deering residence.

The house Prince Jonah Kūhiō Kalaniana'ole built at Ke'alohilani, the beachfront property of Lili'uokalani, on Kalākaua Avenue, at Lili'uokalani Avenue. In June 1918 Kūhiō obtained this land as part of an out of court settlement of his challenge to the legitimacy of the Queen's will and the establishment of the Lili'uokalani Trust.

A reflection of a renewed faith in Hawai'i's stability, resulting from the annexation of the Islands by the United States in 1898, these major architectural statements were joined by others as the century progressed. The George Beckley's built at the foot of Diamond Head their large stone colonial style residence in 1912, and in the ensuing years Prince Kūhiō had his seaside residence, Pualeilani, constructed adjacent to Queen Lili'uokalani's former pier. International Harvester millionaire C.W. Case Deering built his home further down the beach at Kapi'olani Park, and the Dillinghams built La Pietra on the slopes of Diamond Head.

37

Paradise of the Pacific *in 1922 noted that this home was the last space that remained to the royal family in Waikīkī, and predicted, "In time that [house], too, shall become forfeit to the Moloch of modernism, and Waikīkī, for the Hawaiians, will be only a memory." This prophecy proved all too true. After the royal couple's occupancy concluded, the residence housed "a succession of tea rooms", and eventually fell into "dark vacancy". In 1935 the City and County of Honolulu purchased the property at auction and in the following year demolished the house and Liliʻuokalani's pier as part of a beach improvement program.*

Princess Elizabeth Kahanu Kaʻauwai Kalaniana'ole at home. The daughter of a Maui chief, she married Prince Kūhiō on 8 October 1896, upon his release from imprisionment for the role he played in the aborted counterrevolution.

The Living Room of Pualeilani. These interior photographs were taken on Prince Kūhiō's silver wedding anniversary in October 1921, when the house was adorned with silver moss and silver sword.

A lushly planted atrium separated the living and dining rooms of Kūhiō's residence. As Hawai'i's representative to Congress from 1903 until his death in 1922, and the person most responsible for the passsage of the Hawaiian Home Lands legislation, Prince Kūhiō entertained numerous dignitaries at this house, called Pualeilani after Queen Kapi'olani's Waikīkī cottage, which he sold.

Walter F. Dillingham: La Pietra and Polo in the Park

On 4 October 1919, Walter F. Dillingham purchased at auction 9.046 acres on the Waikīkī slope of Diamond Head from the James Campbell Estate for $11,000. On this land, the former site of Papaʻenaʻena *heiau*, he erected a palatial home designed by David Adler, the architect of numerous grand mansions in the Chicago area, including those built for the Armours, McCormicks, and Marshall Field. After its completion in 1922, this house served as the hub of Honolulu social life for over forty years. Presidents, nobility and many other notables enjoyed the the Dillinghams' hospitality, and their home's old world elegance.

Considered at the time of his death to be "the foremost financier and industrialist" in Hawaiʻi, Dillingham was born in Honolulu on 5 April 1875, the eldest son of Benjamin F. and Emma Louise Dillingham. He quit Harvard after two years to assume a clerk position with the Oʻahu Railway and Land Company, and in 1904 took over the management of the company, when his father fell ill. The young man molded his father's debt-ridden empire into a financially sound institution, and upon the elder Dillingham's death in 1918, he became president of this firm.

Besides managing the O.R. & L., Ben Dillingham also headed Hawaiian Dredging Company, which he had organized and incorporated in 1902. The fill from its many dredging projects added over 5,000 acres of land to Hawaiʻi, including 645 acres in Waikīkī and McCully-Moʻiliʻili, the result of their construction of the Ala Wai Canal.

Walter F. Dillingham

La Pietra, the home of Mr. and Mrs. Walter F. Dillingham, was built on the side of Diamond Head in 1921 for an estimated $400,000. It was patterned after Mrs. Dillingham's aunt's villa of the same name in Florence, Italy, where the Dillinghams had been married in 1910. Later Dillingham subdivided the lands ʻEwa of La Pietra to form Noela Place. He had difficulty selling lots in this now fashionable neighborhood, as it was considered to be too hot and dry a location.

La Pietra's dining room.

Socially Dillingham belonged to the Pacific Club, the O'ahu Country Club and the Chamber of Commerce, but his passion was polo. He helped found the Hawai'i Polo and Racing Club and was responsible for bringing polo to Kapi'olani Park, having organized the first interisland polo tournament at the park in 1902. The O'ahu team of A.W. Judd, R.W. Shingle, Dillingham, and C.S. Dole, won this initial tournament for the Wichman Cup. Dillingham captained many victorious polo teams, including a number that went to the mainland to play, and one with his three sons—Gaylord, Lowell and Ben—which was never defeated.

One of many Dillingham captained polo teams at Kapi'olani Park. This team included, from left to right, Walter Macfarlane, Walter Dillingham, Harold Castle, Robert Atkinson.

41

Kapiʻolani Park

*B*esides visiting the beach, various royal residences, or some vestiges of a bygone era, people went to Waikīkī to relax and enjoy themselves at Kapiʻolani Park. With approximately 170 acres of open space, much of which was landscaped, and its race track, and still later polo field, the park remained for most of the nineteenth century "the only park Honolulu can boast of".

Named in honor of King Kalākaua's consort, the park officially opened with an enormous celebration on Kamehameha Day, 11 June 1877. An estimated five to eight thousand people gathered in the park, and the *Pacific Commercial Advertiser* reported:

> *From an early hour the stream of carriages and horsemen with here and there a pedestrian poured out of the city towards Kapiʻolani Park, until by half-past nine the city was pretty much deserted and wore an aspect of Sabbath-like peace and stillness, all shops and places of business being closed and everybody "out of town".*

The crowd listened to speeches delivered by the King and others, and enjoyed a day of horse and foot racing, greased pole climbing, and general festivity. The only disappointment was the lack of waves which led to the cancellation of the scheduled *heʻe nalu* [surf riding].

The park came into existence thanks to the efforts of James Makee, Thomas Cummins, Archibald Cleghorn, and others who organized the Kapiʻolani Park Association in 1876. Chartered to adorn and put in order "a tract of land in the vicinity of Honolulu as a place of public resort", and promote "Agricultural and Stock Exhibitions, and healthful exercise, recreation and amusements", this group received a thirty year lease from King Kalākaua for lands in the area traditionally known as Kāneloa and Kapua.

Bridge leading to the Park, circa 1880. The sign over the entry reads: "Driving faster than a walk over this bridge will be prosecuted according to law".

Kapi'olani Park, circa 1910.

To raise money to develop the park, two hundred shares in the Association were sold at fifty dollars each. Every share gave its subscriber the right to lease a beachfront house lot in the park, and as a result a number of residences were built along the park's shores during the 1880s. With the overthrow of the monarchy in 1893, and the advent of the Republic, many of these prime parcels found their way into private, fee simple ownership.

The revenues generated by the sale of the shares allowed the Association to plant over one thousand trees, channel streams, and construct walks, drives, and a mile long track for horse races. Although compromised by the draining of the streams in the 1920s and the construction of Monsarrat Avenue in the 1930s, this initial park plan remained generally unmodified until after World War II when the City and County of Honolulu implemented a major park improvement program.

Camp McKinley, 1898, the first U.S. Army post in Hawai'i. On 16 August 1898, four days after the annexation of Hawai'i by the United States, the First New York Volunteer Infantry Regiment landed in Honolulu. After some negotiations, the Kapi'olani Park Association granted them permission to establish a temporary camp in the park. The agreed upon two or three day occupancy grew into an encampment which lasted several months. Military encroachment on the park terminated when the Army outraged the Park Association by demanding, among other things, that the canals be drained as they were falsely assumed to be breeding grounds for malaria-carrying mosquitoes. The army eventually vacated their pastoral camp ground, leaving it in ill repair. A hearing held on 30 November, 1898, ruled that the Army had to pay the Park Association $3,175 for the repair of damages to the fences race track, and road ways.

43

Turn-of-the-century views of Makee Island and its surrounding environs, where the Honolulu Zoo is presently located. The construction of the Ala Wai Canal transformed this section of the park from a scenic waterway into a mire of mud.

44

One of the several roads which wound through the watery landscape of Kapi'olani Park, circa 1903.

The Honolulu Aquarium was developed as an attraction at the terminus of the Honolulu Rapid Transit line. It opened on 19 March 1904, and owed much to the generosity of Mr. James Castle who donated the land it stood on; Mr. and Mrs. C.M. Cooke who paid for the construction of the building; and the Honolulu Rapid Transit Company which agreed to stock and maintain the aquarium. Within a month of its opening the aquarium boasted three hundred and fifty fish, representing over eighty varieties. Designed by W.E. Pinkham, this picturesque, vaguely oriental style, lava rock building was razed following the completion of the present aquarium building in 1955.

The bandstand that originally stood on Makee Island.

The lava rock bandstand built in 1926 following a design made by architect Hart Wood. It stood in the same location as the present bandstand, which replaced it in 1968. The outline of the former lily ponds is still visible on the lawn.

47

"A town without a zoo is like a tramp without a can," or so declared E. J. Botts in the December 1917 Paradise of the Pacific. Presumably Honolulu was such a town until the arrival of an elephant called Daisy on 6 September 1916. Honolulu's zoo had existed since early 1915, when Ben Hollinger, head of the City and County's parks committee, began collecting animals; but, the collection was modest and mostly of birds. The drama of Daisy's debut sparked a new interest in the fledgling zoo and gave the endeavor credibility.

The 2,500 pound, three year old pachyderm had been lassoed in Rhodesia by Ellis J. Joseph, who brought her along with a collection of other African and Australian animals to Honolulu in August 1916, on his steamer, Niagara. Her sister had also been captured by Joseph, but unfortunately had not survived the first leg of the 20,000 mile journey which brought Daisy to Honolulu.

Hollinger immediately set out to acquire the magnificent beast, and was able to raise two-thirds of the required $3,000 by soliciting $250 donations from various business houses. Receiving this cash on his day of departure, Joseph promised to return to unload the elephant in September after completing his voyage to Vancouver. Upon Niagara's return, Hollinger received not only the little elephant, but also two kangaroos which Joseph generously donated to the zoo. Bedecked with lei, trunk swaying and big ears flapping, Daisy's journey to Kapiʻolani Park resulted in a miniature parade up Fort Street and out Hotel Street.

At the park Daisy was a sensation. Her official public presentation on 10 September 1916, "displaced polo as the principal attraction at Kapiʻolani Park". Families, eager to see her, crowded onto streetcars and converged on Waikīkī. Erroneously reported to be one of only a dozen elephants in captivity, Daisy was nevertheless the first elephant to set foot in Hawaiʻi, affording many people their initial glimpse of such a creature in the flesh. People enthusiastically predicted that the pachyderm would live for over a hundred years, and the great-grandchildren of current riders would enjoy the pleasure of her company. Such, however, was not Daisy's destiny.

The Parks Board had difficulty properly tending Daisy and with time she became ill-tempered. A move was made during the 1920s to sell her to an American zoo or circus, but public opposition defeated this scheme. She frequently was chained closely to trees for several months at a time, and by 1933 it was reported that the zookeepers feared her and refused to clean her area or give her food and water. As a result, in February 1933, the 'bored' Honolulu Board of Supervisors, following the recommendations of the Parks Board and the 'over-zealous' Humane Society, voted to have Daisy executed in order to put her out of her misery and preclude any potential menace to public safety. This decision aroused public indignation and a storm of protests. A campaign was begun to raise funds to build an adequate compound to house her, and a sixty-day stay of execution was granted. Her original keeper, the 69-year-old George Conradt, volunteered to care for the elephant free of charge, declaring, "If they shoot Daisy, they'll have to shoot me first."

Three days after Conradt resumed his duties, on the afternoon of 3 March 1933, Daisy unexpectedly picked him up with her trunk and gored him on her tusks, killing him instantly. Police marksmen with high powered rifles were called to the scene, and after receiving repeated bullets to the head the bewildered beast fell over dead in a puddle of water.

Two wallabies, who also accompanied Daisy on her journey to Hawaiʻi, met with a more fortuitous fate. The day after their purchase by Richard H. Trent, they escaped from his private zoo on ʻAlewa Heights. Their descendants still populate the Koʻolau mountains in the back of Kalihi valley.

Daisy's arrival in Honolulu.

To help defray Daisy's purchase price, children were charged five cents to ride, four at a time, on "her amply swaying back".

Ben Hollinger holding Daisy by her "affectionate and very inquisitive trunk."

49

The War Memorial Natatorium in the late 1930s. Built as a monument to Hawai'i's World War I dead, the natatorium officially opened on 24 August 1927, with an AAU national championship meet which included swimmers from Japan and South America. Former Olympic champion Duke Kahanamoku took the first plunge and in the competition that followed. John Weissmuller established new world records in the 100, 400, and 880 meter freestyles. Clarence 'Buster' Crabbe, a local swimmer who later replaced Weissmuller in the Tarzan series, won the 1500 meter contest.

50

The Phoenix Fountian was built with moneys raised by Hawai'i's Japanese community on 10 November 1915, the coronation day of Emperor Yoshihito. Designed and constructed by the Tokyo Art Academy, it resembled a similar fountain in Tokyo's Hibiya Park. Dedicated on 16 March 1919, the fountain's bronze plaque proclaimed:

Here meet the culture of East and West: the Hope of Human Brotherhood is Best Erected by the Japanese in Hawai'i in commemoration of the accesion to the throne of Nippon, in November, 1915, of the 123rd emperor and presented by them to the City and County of Honolulu, in token of their love and affection for the land of their residence, the Paradise of the Pacific.

A casuality of the war, the fountain fell on 14 December 1942, to the public's indignant cries against imperialist imagery, one year and seven days after the bombing of Pearl Harbor. The City and County of Honolulu erected a more modest fountain on the site of the former Phoenix Fountain in 1950. That fountain was replaced in 1967 by the Mrs. Walter F. Dillingham Memorial Fountain.

Bathhouses and Hostelries

Although described in tourist literature as the Brighton, Newport, or Trouville of Hawai'i, nineteenth century Waikīkī offered visitors little in the way of resort facilities. Primarily a sedate residential area, accessible only through friends and letters of introduction, this world famous beach functioned essentially as a day-use playground for the citizens of Honolulu. Those people who ventured there in search of customary resort activities were bound for disappointment, for as Charles Nottage noted in 1894, "With the exception of a few unpretentious cottages, there is not the remotest sign of its [Waikīkī's] being a watering place. A wooden shed, in which one can undress, is called, so the guide-book assures me, 'The Long Branch Baths'."

Bathhouses, such as the Long Branch, were one of the few enterprises in Waikīkī to cater to visitors. In return for a fee, these commercial ventures offered bathers a towel, bathing suit, dressing rooms and a stretch of beach and ocean to enjoy. According to the May 1892, *Paradise of the Pacific*:

> *Here the tourist may lave in the warm waters of the tropical Pacific and enjoy a bath which has no superior for comfort and pleasure in any portion of the wide, wide world. At times the surf rolls in in magnificent breakers and the grandeur of such times needs to be seen to be appreciated.*

Waikīkī circa 1890. In the background the Long Branch's marine toboggan extends into the ocean.

Waikīkī Beach, in the late 1890s. The white building at the ocean edge is the Long Branch Baths. The pier in the background was built by W.C. Peacock in the 1890s, and later served the Moana Hotel, built by Peacock in 1901.

52

The earliest known Waikīkī bathhouse, the Long Branch, was named after the then popular New Jersey resort where Presidents Grant, Hayes, Garfield, and Arthur had maintained summer White Houses. James Dodd, the owner of the Pantheon Saloon and Livery Stables, established the baths in 1881 at Ulukou, the former residence of Kākuhihewa. Along with the baths he operated an 'omnibus' or carriage service to Waikīkī and offered the public a special fifty-cent roundtrip fare which included admission to the Long Branch.

By 1889 the Long Branch boasted forty-two "dressing rooms for gentlemen" and eighteen "boudoirs for ladies". In that year proprietor James Sherwood added forty rooms to accommodate the anticipated rush in business to result from his construction of a "marine toboggan" on the site. Modeled after a similar attraction in Bridgeport, Connecticut, the toboggan was enjoyed by both men and women, and the *Pacific Commercial Advertiser* advised its readers that, "this pastime cannot be otherwise than delightful and it gives an excitement which ordinary bathing lacks."

Besides the Long Branch, other, less exhilarating, bathing pavilions also dotted the shores of Waikīkī. Diamond Head of the Long Branch , the Ilaniwai Baths and Wright's Villa stood at what is now called Kūhiō Beach. Both opened around 1895, the former under the management of a carpenter, William Stevens, and the latter under the management of a blacksmith, Thomas Wright. The Waikīkī Beach Company, Ltd. gained possession of these two parcels in October 1899. It removed the bathhouses at Ilaniwai and developed the entire property into a more substantial hotel complex. The company named their new venture the Waikīkī Inn, a name which would be associated with these premises off and on for the next sixty years.

The two-hundred-foot-long marine toboggan at the Long Beach Baths rose forty feet above the high tide mark and featured a twenty-inch-wide chute with wooden rollers. For a nickel, riders could climb a ladder to the top of the run, mount a 'star oval board', zip down the chute and "ricochet across the water . . ., skipping along like a flat pebble." A good ride took a person about 75 to 150 feet out from the shore, according to the Daily Bulletin *of 17 May 1889.*

The Waikīkī Villa, or Hawaiian Annex, circa 1895, which Paradise of the Pacific *described as a "very commodious and elegant bathhouse". One of the few bathhouses to have lodging facilities, this building contained four apartments for overnight guests.*

On the other side of the Long Branch, at the present premises of the Sheraton Waikīkī, stood the Waikīkī Villa. Hamilton Johnson established this bathhouse in 1889 to serve as a beach annex for his downtown hotel, the Hamilton House. Two years later Johnson opened the bathhouse's doors to guests of Honolulu's foremost hotel, the Hawaiian, when he became manager and part-owner of that downtown hostelry. While associated with the Hawaiian, the Waikīkī Villa became known as the Hawaiian Annex and an elaborate oceanfront pavilion was built.

'Ewa of the Waikīkī Villa, at the approximate location of today's Reef Hotel, stood the Saratoga Baths. Named after the hot springs resort in upstate New York, it remained in operation for most of the 1890s, and, more than likely, bestowed its name upon Saratoga Street, the main thoroughfare between the baths and the tramway stop on Waikīkī Road.

Further down the beach, at the present site of the Hilton Hawaiian Village, stood yet another bathhouse, the Old Waikīkī. It commenced operations in 1891, offering visitors room and board as well as ocean bathing. This establishment had a short life, and in 1895 John and Eliza Cassidy purchased the property. Here they maintained a boarding house, which in 1911 became a hotel, Cassidy's 'At the Beach'.

During the late nineteenth century the bathhouses serviced the needs of the majority of visitors interested in recreating at Waikīkī. A few baths, such as Wright's Villa, the Hawaiian Annex, and the Old Waikīkī, offered a limited number of rooms for overnight guests, but the demand for such accommodations was small. However, as the allure of Waikīkī as a bathing resort grew, so too did the possibility of establishing a viable hotel in the area. As early as 1881 the *Hawaiian Gazette* wondered at the fact that no hotel had been started in Waikīkī, but only two notable attempts were made in this direction during the waning decades of the 1800s, and neither met with great success.

The first hotel on the beach at Waikīkī opened seven months after the January 1888 *Paradise of the Pacific* commented that, "As yet there is no hotel to meet the wants of the public at Waikīkī." Its proprietor, C.N. Arnold, leased Colonel George W. Macfarlane's sprawling Kapi'olani Park estate, located where the current Elk's Club stands, and converted this fine residence into the Park Beach Hotel. This establishment contained ten bedrooms, with gas and water in each, as well as a stable and carriage house with an "upper floor fitted with large airy rooms, suitable for servants, etc." Other amenities included a bathhouse, billiard table, bowling alley, and a table "supplied with the best the market affords". Claiming the "finest bathing on the Islands," Arnold conscientiously catered to the tourist trade. He advertised that "buses and baggage wagons will meet every steamer", and that visitors would be provided with "full information . . . as to the best route to travel, for scenery and curiosities; also current rates for horse hire and guides on the other Islands". The Park Beach unfortunately did not survive a year, and in May 1889 Macfarlane put the hotel up for lease. He received no takers, but in December 1889, James B. Castle purchased the property and returned it to residential use.

Night view of the Hawaiian Annex. Here, during the 1890s, Saturday night dancing reputedly was introduced to Honolulu.

The picturesque Park Beach Hotel was originally the residence of George W. Macfarlane. Situated on the land currently occupied by the Elks Club, it is the earliest known Waikīkī beach hotel.

56

The Sans Souci in 1902. "The beau ideal of a summer resort,"Paradise of the Pacific proclaimed, "there is no place on earth to which memory will revert with more pleasurable recollections than this tree-embowered, sun-kissed haven of rest at Waikīkī." Literally translated 'without care', Sans Souci was the name of Frederick the Great's Potsdam Palace. The Charles J. Hartwell family razed the original Sans Souci and in 1927 replaced it with another house, which served as a residence and boarding house until 1960 when it yielded to the fifteen-story Sans Souci cooperative apartment which stands there today.

The other major nineteenth century Waikīkī hotel venture was the Sans Souci. In 1884 Allen Herbert, who had guided the downtown Hawaiian Hotel through its first ten years of existence (1872–1882), proposed to open his recently acquired seaside residence at Kapi'olani Park "as a family resort and watering place", where "casual visitors" could find room and board. He anticipated that race day and the Agricultural Society's Fair would attract sufficient patrons for such an enterprise, but nothing apparently came of this idea. In 1893, George Lycurgus, who later managed the Hilo Hotel and Volcano House on the island of Hawai'i, opened the Sans Souci Hotel at the former Herbert residence. This oceanside resort had a brief, but illustrious existence. Shortly after its opening, in September–October 1893, Robert Louis Stevenson secured an eternal niche in the romantic history of Hawai'i for the hotel, by staying there for five weeks during his second visit to the Islands. Upon his departure from the hotel, he wrote in the ledger, "If anyone desires such old-fashioned things as lovely scenery, quiet, pure air, clear sea water, good food, and heavenly sunsets hung out before his eyes over the Pacific and the distant hills of Waianae, I recommend him cordially to the Sans Souci."

The Sans Souci's famous lanai on which Robert Louis Stevenson convalesced during his 1893 stay in Hawai'i.

The Moana Hotel, Waikīkī's first major hotel.

The roof garden at night.

Sculptor Allen Hutchinson, who at the time of Stevenson's visit executed the only known bust of the poet from life, described the Sans Souci as, "truly Bohemian, with no pretense at modern luxury.... The main building was a ramshackle wooden structure, a huge room which served as lounge and dining room combined, called 'lānai' to which the kitchen and offices were attached." In this 'ramshackle' building, supporters of the Queen plotted to restore the monarchy, but their hopes were dashed in January 1895, when the Republic decisively squelched their counterrevolution. In February 1895, Lycurgus was charged with treason for his support of the royalist cause, but these charges, along with those brought against many other people, were later dropped. The Sans Souci remained in operation for several more years but closed before the turn of the century when Alexander Hawes, the new owner of the property, decided to use it as a private residence.

So ended the early endeavors to develop a hotel industry in Waikīkī. With the closing of the Sans Souci, Waikīkī was again without any formal hotel facilities. It remained so until March 11, 1901, when the Moana Hotel opened its doors to the public and a new age.

Developed by the Moana Hotel Company, a local corporation headed by W.C. Peacock, the Moana was big and beautiful, "the costliest and most elaborate hotel building in the Hawaiian Islands". Although built of wood, its main body rose a full four stories above the street, and a fifth story roof garden further accentuated its height. At the time of its completion, it was one of the tallest buildings in Honolulu with only the Stangenwald Block exceeding it in height. From its roof garden, the earliest known in the Islands, guests obtained a panoramic view of almost the entire city, and this magnificent vantage point became the setting for many social events including numerous banquets and receptions.

The Moana was a sight to behold. Through its Ionic-columned porte cochere, arcaded front porch, second and fourth story balconies, and embellished frieze and window frames, architect Oliver G. Traphagen handsomely translated the then-current Beaux Arts style of architecture into wood. Delightfully open and airy, the building followed no Mainland format, but instead was built expressly as a resort hotel for Hawai'i. Thoroughly modern, it had its own electrical plant and an elevator, and each of the seventy-five rooms included a bath and telephone. To say the least, it was the most impressive building in Waikīkī. Its commanding presence dominated the beach in a manner surpassed only by Diamond Head.

The hotel got off to an auspicious start when over one hundred Shriners stepped off the *S.S. Sierra* and checked into the new hostelry on 12 March 1901. Their arrival presaged a new era in Waikīkī's history in which hotels and visitors would come to play an expanding role as the years passed. Between 1900 and 1917, the number of tourists that came to Hawai'i each year steadily grew from approximately 3,000 to

The Moana circa 1907. Here, at beach level beneath the dining room was located the Hui Nalu Beach Boys Club, to which Duke Kahanamoku belonged. The former Long Branch Bathhouse stands on the beach to the left of the hotel.

The banyan courtyard from which 'Hawai'i Calls' was broadcast for so many years.

LOUNGE—MOANA HOTEL
HONOLULU

The lounge in the Moana Hotel.

In need of repairs, the Moana's three-hundred-foot pier was torn down in 1930 because it was deemed a hazard. The prominent structure on the left is the hotel dining room.

Concrete wings, completed in 1918 at a cost of $530,000, more than double the hotel's capacity by adding one hundred rooms.

over 8,000 by the outbreak of World War I. An increasing number of these people sought out Waikīkī accommodations rather than remain in downtown Honolulu, the traditional resting place of travelers to the Islands.

With the Moana Hotel, Waikīkī emerged as a hospitable resort destination and, in the ensuing years, a number of more modest, cottage-style hotels opened for business. The best known of these, the Honolulu Seaside, commenced operation in 1906, when the former owner of the long-departed Park Beach Hotel's premises, George W. Macfarlane, gained possession of the Hawaiian Annex bathhouse and its adjoining parcel, the royal coconut grove, Helumoa. The hotel was comprised of a number of cottages and tent houses which were scattered over the approximately ten-acre beach-front site. The magnificent Hawaiian Annex bathhouse remained on the premises and was a favorite haunt of the hotel's guests. The Seaside advertised its beach as "the finest part of the most delightful bathing beach in the world", and the management further proclaimed that it was "strictly a high-class hotel in every respect", the patronage of which "includes the best people of the country". Such claims as well as the charming grounds, certainly helped promote the hotel, and during its formative years the Seaside could claim Alice Roosevelt and Jack and Charmaine London among its satisfied customers.

The main drive of the Seaside Hotel.

In the foreground people gather on the spacious oceanside grounds of the Honolulu Seaside Hotel. The building on the grounds to the left, is the former residence of Charles R. and Bernice Pauahi Bishop.

Jack London and his wife, Charmain, frequented the Seaside during November 1915, the author's last stay in the Islands.

The Honolulu Seaside Hotel. In 1906, George W. Macfarlane sponsored a contest with a ten dollar prize to name the hotel he intended to open at Helumoa. He received over 400 entries which ranged in appropriateness from the Wainani [beautiful waters] and the Maluhia [place of rest]—both of which were strongly considered—to the Kameamaoli [the real thing], Niulaalani [sacred coconuts of heaven], and Malu-Auinala [afternoon shade], and to the more trite Dew Drop Inn, Minnehaha, and Spread Eagle Hotel. No one submitted the name finally chosen, the Honolulu Seaside Hotel, but Mr. S.L. Peleiholani was awarded the ten dollars for his entry, the Honolulu.

63

The Seaside was early Waikīkī's most
glorious cottage style hotel. In 1925, when its
grounds were cleared in preparation for the
building of the Royal Hawaiian Hotel, the
Honolulu Advertiser eulogized:

Her household of memories scattered to
the long tradewinds, Romance, evicted
from her dwellings, wanders homeless
at Waikīkī. Time and Change, stern
inn keepers, struck her name from the
register of the Seaside Hotel when work
of demolishing and removing the old
hotel buildings was brought under way.

Some of the hotel fell to the wrecker's hands,
while other of its cottages were moved to the
present site of the Princess Kaiulani Hotel,
where they were used as visitor
accommodation until after World War II.

Alice Roosevelt, the daughter of President
Theodore Roosevelt, visited Hawai'i in 1905
enroute to Manila with Secretary of War
William Howard Taft to study America's
defense of the Pacific. She went surfriding in
an outrigger canoe at the Moana Hotel one
afternoon, and "regaled herself to the limit in
this exhilarating pastime". In 1907 she
returned with her husband, Nicholas
Longworth, for a one month stay. Their
cottage at the Seaside became a hub of social
life and, on 4 September 1907, they invited
two hundred guests to a formal farewell party
which Paradise of the Pacific declared to be
"the most illustrious social event of the
season, if not of the past year". While in
Hawai'i, Alice Roosevelt also managed to
shock the community by smoking cigarettes
in public.

Teatime at the Seaside.

The Longworth cottage.

The Macfarlanes of Waikīkī

*I*n 1846, Harry and Eliza Macfarlane arrived in Honolulu from New Zealand. They settled in Waikīkī in the area where the International Market Place now holds sway, and planted the large banyan tree that stands there today. They raised six children, and the family has provided a legacy in the fields of visitor accommodations and water sports at Waikīkī.

The firstborn, George W. Macfarlane (1849-1921), was an energetic and personable man, who successfully involved himself in a variety of enterprises, including the sugar, hotel, importing and wholesale liquor businesses. He became a wealthy man, and his stature was further enhanced by his friendship with David Kalākaua, whom he had known since childhood. When Kalākaua ascended to the Hawaiian throne, Macfarlane was appointed to the king's personal staff with the rank of Colonel. He took an active role in the politics of Kalākaua's reign, and was the youngest person appointed to the House of Nobles.

Considered "one of the shrewdest businessmen in Honolulu", people frequently called upon Colonel Macfarlane to represent them in financial transactions. Through such a role he was responsible for the conception of many sugar enterprises, including Claus Spreckles' sugar empire on Maui. He also negotiated one of the greatest financial accomplishments of his time when he obtained for the Kingdom a two million dollar loan from Great Britain.

Colonel G. W. Macfarlane accompanied King Kalāukaua on his trip around the world in 1881, and in 1888 was made the king's Chamberlain. This appointment came seven months after Macfarlane and F. H. Hayselden were convicted of defrauding the government of duties on 'election gin' they had distributed for the King prior to the elections of 1886. As Chamberlain, Macfarlane traveled with the King to San Francisco, and was at Kalākaua's bedside at the time of the monarch's death on 20 January 1891.

Commodore Clarence W. Macfarlane's yacht La Paloma *which won the first Trans-Pacific Yacht Race in 1906. Returning to Hawai'i shortly after the San Francisco earthquake, the yacht went slightly off course, and the crew feared the worst for the Islands when at first they could not find them.*

The thatched house in Waikīkī where the newly wed Fred and Emilie Macfarlane first lived.

Walter J. Macfarlane

Colonel C.H. Judd, King Kalākaua and Colonel G.W. Macfarlane.

Colonel G.W. Macfarlane recurringly was associated, either directly or indirectly, with the development of the hotel industry in Waikīkī. His Waikīkī estate in Kapi'olani Park, leased to G.N. Arnold in 1888, became the Park Beach Hotel, the first known oceanside hostelry in Waikīkī. Under Macfarlane's ownership of the downtown Royal Hawaiian Hotel, Hamilton Johnson was made a partner and manager. He, in turn, made his beachfront bathhouse available as the Royal Hawaiian Hotel's Waikīkī Annex. Macfarlane later gained control over this property, and it became the Honolulu Seaside Hotel. When George left Honolulu in 1910 to live out his life on the US east coast, his brother, Clarence (1858-1947), who claimed to be the first white person in Honolulu to master the sport of surf boarding and canoeing in outriggers, managed the Seaside. The youngest in the family, Commodore Clarence Macfarlane was best known as the founder of the Trans-Pacific Yacht Race.

Another brother with close ties to Waikīkī was Frederick W. Macfarlane (1853-1929), who was president of the Union Feed Company and operated a pineapple plantation at Ahuimanu. Fred married Emilie Widemann on 5 April 1879, and the young couple lived in a thatched house on Waikīkī beach for a year prior to building a more substantial dwelling on the site. Located on the Honolulu side of the Seaside Hotel, next to the Wilders, Fred and 'Auntie Mela' resided here all their lives. Their son, F. Walter Macfarlane played polo regularly in Kapi'olani Park, and their grandson, Walter J. Macfarlane (1907-1943) was an active water sports participant, who died tragically of typhoid at the age of 36. A month after his death the Outrigger Canoe Club honored Walter, who had for many years served as the club's president, by holding the Fourth of July Walter J. Macfarlane Memorial Canoe races at Waikīkī beach. This has become the longest running canoe event in Hawai'i.

67

WAIKIKI INN

WAIKIKI BEACH, HONOLULU

BEST PART OF THE BEACH FOR **BATHING**

FINE HOTEL, CAFE AND BUFFET ACCOMMODATIONS

TAKE KING
STREET CARS **W. C. BERGIN, PROP.**

TELEPHONE
838

There were a number of other progeny of the bathhouse era which expanded their operations with the new century. These all tended to have a high turnover of ownership and frequent name changes. The Waikīkī Inn grew in size during the opening years of the decade, but fell into hard times in 1915, and was sold to Rudolf Heydenreich. It became known as Heinies Tavern for the next few years, until it ran into economic straits with the coming of prohibition. Then for a year or two the Elks used the property as a lodgehall, and in 1923 Rawley's Ice Cream and Dairy Products assumed the lease. Under this firm the Waikīkī Inn name was reinstituted and within several years of their takeover the hotel again resumed full services.

Similarly Cassidy's At the Beach underwent several changes during this period. In 1914 its name was changed to the Pierpoint, and in 1922 J.F. Child purchased the hotel. He used it as the oceanside annex for his downtown Blaisdell Hotel until 1927 when he sold it to the Heen Investment Company which improved the facilities and renamed it the Niumalu Hotel.

A couple of other modest hotels, the Hau Tree and Gray's By-the-Sea, stood on the beach between the newly developed Fort DeRussy and the Seaside Hotel. The latter opened in 1913 when Mrs. Lavancha Gray, the former manager of the Pleasanton Hotel in Makiki, leased the two-story residence of Minnie and Joe Gilman. To the town side of Gray's stood the Hau Tree, which had commenced business in 1907 when Honolulu newspaperman Edward Irwin leased Robert Lewers' beachfront house at

The Lewers residence (far right) as it appeared in 1914, then under the management of Mrs. Cecilia N. Arnold. At that time it was called the Hau Tree.

The J.A. Gilman residence in 1908; this later became Gray's By-the-Sea.

68

the foot of what today is Lewers Street. He converted the two-story house into a small hotel, the Hau Tree, named after the trees which so grandly sheltered its lānai. Within several years Irwin subleased the establishment to Cecilia N. Arnold, the widow of the former proprietor of the Park Beach Hotel.

With the expiration of Irwin's lease in 1917, Clifford Kimball, the manager of the Hale'iwa Hotel, the O.R.&L.'s major passanger terminus on O'ahu's north shore, took over the Hau Tree. He changed the name to the Halekūlani [house befitting heaven], which derived from an earlier time when the Lewers family had allowed Hawaiians to beach and store their canoes in the area between the house and the ocean. It was these grateful paddlers who originally bestowed the name upon the dwelling.

Kimball increased the Halekūlani's capacity by placing a number of guest cottages on the property in 1920. In 1924 he further expanded by purchasing the property of Arthur M. Brown, and in 1928 he bought the Gilman parcel which contained Gray's By-the-Sea. After Kimball's purchase, Gray's remained in operation until the expiration of Mrs. Gray's lease in 1931. The hotel then moved to the adjoining property, but remained in this location for only one year before closing in 1932 when Kimball also incorporated this land into the Halekūlani's grounds.

In addition to the more stable operations discussed above, a number of small hotels had fleeting existences in Waikīkī during the opening decades of the twentieth century. Two deserve mention: 'Āinahau, the former residence of Princess Ka'iulani, and the hotel located near the Waikīkī Inn at 2517 Kalākaua Avenue. Mrs. E.H. Lewis operated 'Āinahau as a small private hotel from 1913 to 1917 when the property was subdivided for residential purposes after city officials declined the donation of the estate as a public park.

In 1912, prior to running 'Āinahau, Mrs. Lewis opened the Sea Beach Hotel at 2517 Kalākaua Avenue. This property went through a series of proprietors and names before going out of business in about 1925. Following Mrs. Lewis's move to 'Āinahau,

Snapping a 1922 view of Diamond Head from the 'Ewa end of the Halekūlani seawall.

'Āinahau as a hotel, circa 1915.

The Hau Tree's lānai. In 1917 this cottage hotel came under the proprietorship of Clifford Kimball and was renamed the Halekūlani Hotel.

the hotel became the Beach House under the direction of Mrs. Thomas McVeagh. It remained so for two years, and then, for another two years, under the management of Nelson Ware, its name was Hawaiianized to the Hale Kai. In 1917, Mrs. Fred Whitney acquired the property and for eight years used it as the Waikīkī annex of her Roselawn Hotel. With the demise of the Roselawn, this property was absorbed by the expanding Waikīkī Inn.

Thus, the opening decades of the twentieth century saw Waikīkī change from an area primarily residential in character to one dotted with thriving hotels. Claiming no hotels in 1899, by 1919 Waikīkī could boast of five major hostelries: the Moana, Seaside, Halekūlani, Pierpoint, and Waikīkī Inn. Despite such development, Waikīkī was still not the visitor center of Hawai'i. The combined guest capacity of these five operations was almost equaled by that of the three hundred room Alexander Young Hotel in downtown Honolulu. As a focus for the tourist industry, Waikīkī, although growing, was yet in its infancy. However, the "watering place" claims made by the tourist literature were approaching realization.

71

Activity in the Midst of Tranquility

Kalākaua Avenue from the top of the Moana Hotel, circa 1920. The Honolulu Rapid Transit Company's trolleys serviced Waikīkī from 1903 to 1941, when they were replaced by bus service.

*I*n addition to new hotels and residences, the initial years of the twentieth century witnessed other changes in the Waikīkī landscape. On 1 February 1903, the Honolulu Rapid Transit Company inaugurated service between downtown and Waikīkī, and reduced the time to commute between the two districts from 45 to 28 minutes. To celebrate the event, the company offered free passage on opening day, and the *Pacific Commercial Advertiser* estimated that "almost every resident of the city was carried over the line at some time or another during the day". The newspaper went on to state:

> *Everyone in Honolulu went to the beach yesterday. The Moana, the Waikīkī Inn, the Annex, all the beach resorts, felt the impetus of this travel beachward, and the park was full of people all day . . . Honolulu felt, indeed, that Waikīkī had at last become part of itself, and the dwellers by the surges knew that their long isolation was at an end.*

Waikīkī increasingly became a focal point for social and recreational activities for a larger and larger segment of Honolulu's population. The Rapid Transit Company not only provided easier access to the area, but also brought to Waikīkī the aquarium as an end-of-the-line attraction. Other recreation oriented facilities also grew up along the beach to meet the needs of the populace. In 1907 a public bathhouse was erected in

A crowd turned out at Sans Souci in December 1902 to witness the arrival of the trans-Pacific cable. The house on the point in the background is that of James B. Castle.

74

The public baths and beach at Kapi'olani Park were built by the City & County of Honolulu in 1907 (left and middle left). The insert shows the keeper of the bath house, J. K. Nahaolelua.

Kapi'olani Park, and in the following year Alexander Hume Ford catalyzed the founding of the Hawaiian Outrigger Canoe Club. Located on an acre and a half of land situated between the Seaside and Moana hotels, the club originally was conceived as an organization to revitalize the 'royal sport' of surfing on boards and in outrigger canoes, by providing 'the small boy of limited means' access to the beach.

In its earlier years the club also encouraged young women to surf, and Ruth Soper and Bishop Restarick's daughter, Margaret, were the first female members of the Outrigger to, respectively, stand on a surf board and ride a wave all the way to shore.

Along with encouraging the perpetuation of ocean related sports, the Outrigger Canoe Club also had a social aspect which grew with the passing years. By the 1930s the club had become one of the more prestigious and exclusive organizations in the territory, and in 1941 its new clubhouse was dedicated to not only the "promotion and preservation of Hawaiian aquatic sports", but also to "the encouragement of social activites in congenial surroundings".

The entry to the Hawaiian Outrigger Canoe Club. A thatch-roofed pavilion stands on the shore of the muliwai [estuary].

In 1930, this sprawling Hawaiian style structure, designed by Ralph E. Fishbourne, supplanted the earlier bathhouse, and featured a food concession, dance floor and wading pool. In 1966 the present restrooms and concession replaced this gracious building.

The Outrigger Canoe Club, circa 1909. The thatch houses near the beach were 'authentic Hawaiian grass houses' purchased from a defunct zoo in Kaimukī. They served as a bathhouse and storage shed for canoes and surfboards. To the far left is the Seaside Hotel's pavilion and in the foreground the muliwai fed by 'Āpuakēhau stream, empties into the Pacific Ocean. The houses in the right background are on the mauka [mountain] side of Kalākaua Avenue.

The view from a canoe shed.

*The pavilion-like clubhouse, designed by the
Honolulu architectural firm of Ripley &
Davis, replaced the original cluster of
thatched houses in 1915. In 1925 this facility
was moved* mauka *to accommodate the
Royal Hawaiian Hotel, and in 1939 was
replaced by a more modern structure,
designed by architect C.W. Dickey.
That building was supplanted by the
present Outrigger Hotel in 1964.*

Firing a practice round. The first round fired produced a black smoke, the result of the oil in the barrel burning.

Muster on Kalia Road.

78

Battery Randolph's two fourteen-inch rifles were the largest guns in the Territory. Whenever the Army fired these weapons, the residents in Waikīkī were warned to open doors and windows, and remove china from shelves. The Army had to blast a channel through Waikīkī's reef so a barge could deliver guns with their 69-ton barrels to Fort DeRussy. Completed in 1911, Battery Randolph and the no-longer-extant Battery Dudley were built to defend Honolulu Harbor. Their guns were never fired in anger, and played no role in the defense of Pearl Harbor. In Janaury 1949, the post was designated as an Armed Forces Recreational Area, a function it still fulfills. In 1969 the Army decided to demolish Battery Randolph. However, in the confrontation betweeen wrecking ball and fortification, the ball crumbled. Dynamite was next considered, but munitions experts shied away from such an attempt as they feared the required blast would shatter most of the windows in Waikīkī. Thus, the Army dedicated the seemingly indestructible battery as an Army museum on 7 December 1976.

USGS Map of Waikīkī, 1910, U.S. Army Corps of Engineers, Fort DeRussy.

The most profound change to occur in Waikīkī during the early twentieth century involved the acquisition by the U.S. War Department of approximately 73 acres of the area known as Kālia. The territorial government, led by Governor Sanford B. Dole, strongly opposed this action, claiming that a military installation with loud coastal guns was most undesirable in the midst of a residential section.

Despite such protests, the War Department, between 1904 and 1910, obtained by fee simple purchase, condemnation, and Presidential Executive Order, the Kālia Military Reservation. In 1909 the Department named the new post Fort DeRussy in honor of Brigadier General Rene Edward DeRussy of the Corps of Engineers. General DeRussy had graduated from West Point in 1812, had served in the War of 1812, the Mexican War and the Civil War, and had been responsible for the construction of numerous defenses on both coasts of the United States.

On 12 November 1908, a detachment of the 1st Battalion of Engineers from Fort Mason, California, occupied the new post. A tent camp was established and Major E. Eveleth Winslow, the new Fort's commander, reported that the men were "quite comfortably placed". The officers, however, were "pretty bad off . . . the only quarters the officers were able to find are the shacks on the beach which are in poor condition, with leaky roofs and next to no plumbing." Disenchanted with these one-time summer cottages, Major Winslow took up residence at the Moana Hotel until January 1909, when suitable quarters on the post presumably were arranged for him.

Between 1909 and 1911 the engineers were primarily occupied with mapping the island of O'ahu. At DeRussy other activities also had to be attended to—especially the filling of a portion of the fish ponds which covered most of the Fort. This task fell to the Quartermaster Corps, and they accomplished it through the use of an hydraulic dredger which pumped fill from the ocean continuously for nearly a year in order to build up an area on which permanent structures could be built. Thus the Army began the transformation of Waikīkī from wetlands to solid ground.

DeRussy diving platform. Dredging the ocean bottom for fill to reclaim much of DeRussy's fishponds resulted in a good swimming beach at the Fort.

In the midst of all the dramatic building in Waikīkī, the Catholic Church improved its mission in the area, but did so in a more modest manner with the construction of the 'church without windows' in 1901. The mission was founded in 1854 and remained relatively small until 1898 when Father Valentin H. Franckx was appointed to it. In order to tend the needs of Waikīkī's first major influx of mainland visitors, the soldiers stationed at Camp McKinley in Kapiolani Park, Father Valentin [facing the camera in the photograph] designed this charming "Polynesian Gothic" style church which was dedicated on 25 August 1901.

Although well suited to Hawai'i's environment, this handsome frame structure did not survive Waikīkī's next development frenzy. It was razed in 1961 to make way for the present St. Augustine's church, the largest church in Hawai'i when built.

Mistaking the lights of the Moana Hotel for those leading into Honolulu Harbor, the British barkentine Helga ran aground on the reef off Waikīkī at about 2 AM on 11 August 1910. Approximately 300 yards distant from the beach at Cassidy's, the 209 foot long, three-masted sailing ship remained on the reef for ten days, before the surf completely destroyed it. Commanded by Captain Daniel Wall, the ship was 123 days out of Newcastle, Australia bound for San Francisco with 1,780 tons of coal. The vessel's untimely demise brought many people out to the shallow waters to gather the coal and timbers which heated stoves in many Honolulu kitchens for months to come.

The ship, built in Norway, was launched in 1892 as the Fortuna. Coincidentally, the British bark Fortunio, also out of Newcastle with a load of coal, wrecked on the Waikīkī reef in 1851, approximately 100 feet from the final resting place of the Helga.

81

"Waikīkī beach yesterday was the mecca of
everybody, it seemed, who wanted to get
away from the hot streets and find the cool
spots beneath the waves . . .

'This is one of the best bathing days we
have ever had here,' said Manager Theale of
the Moana. 'It looks as if people are
beginning to realize that sea-bathing is close
at hand and that it is a tonic and saves
doctors' bills.

'Tourists come here and disport themselves
in the water mornings and afternoons almost
daily, and they wonder why so few
Honoluluans patronize the beaches'."

With an increased interest in ocean bathing, younger women revolted against the dictates of fashion and morality, and began to shed the layers of beachwear that encumbered their frolicking in the surf. During the summer of 1913, Sunday bathers at Waikīkī witnessed a progression of brazenness as the summer advanced. Under the assurance of anonymity, a young lady informed the Pacific Commercial Advertiser of her and her six friends' experience of 7 June 1913: "It is no secret around the beach that most of the girls wear boys' bathing suits now, under their top skirts and blouses. Ever since we took up swimming in earnest we have discarded the heavy bloomers and stockings, and we generally swim out to the end of the [Moana Hotel] pier, slip off our skirts and have a real swim out to the reef, leaving our coming out clothes in care of some friend. Well, we did that Saturday and we had a lovely time in the surf. We had such a good time that the girl we left our skirts with got tired and went away, and that started our troubles. Along came some busybody who saw the wet suits lying on the pier, and, of course, gathered them up and took them back to the bathhouse." As the beach was "thick with people" the girls stayed in the water until they got too cold, "then we just had to swim ashore and dash to the dressing rooms with hundreds and hundreds of people rubbering." To say the least, the informant admitted, "we were embarrassed."

By the end of June women had "forsaken stockings" at the beach and the Star-Bulletin presented its readers with a drama starring "two maidens wearing tight-fitting men's bathing suits" on Waikīkī beach: "There is noticeable excitement along the beach at the unusual and fascinating sight. Old women are heard to tell old men that 'it was not like that in the olden days.' And though the old men don't say anything it is made clear by their optic actions that they would rather have one of the present days than a whole assortment of the bygone ones. Young women are seen leading their husbands firmly and blushingly away."

By mid-July the Advertiser reported that one lady, "apparently a stranger to Honolulu", discarded her blouse and stockings under the Moana pier and cavorted in the ocean in "a tight fitting silken suit of brilliant yellow, something the color of a quarantine flag". The "golden mermaid" swam to the reef "followed by a lively school of admiring swimmers". Honolulu Mayor Fern expressed a desire to pass a law similar to that of Atlantic City, forbidding women from wearing "close fitting bathing garb of men". Fern was quoted as saying, "It is certainly wrong and against public morals for young women to appear in men's bathing suits in public. It may be more comfortable for them to swim in than the regular women's suits, but that is not a sufficient excuse." A week later, however, the mayor changed his mind and decided to, "let them have the light suit. Any kind they want they can have, for all of me. I shall not butt-in. It is their business, and if they want a boy's suit let them have it. And anyway, unofficially speaking, just as one citizen to another, a boy's suit is much better looking." It quickly became 'the thing' for young ladies to not only wear men's bathing suits on the beach, but for Waikīkī residents to don such a "low-necked, sleeveless, legless one-piece suit" as this one worn by Gertrude McQueen, and stroll to the beach, exposing "themselves to the scandal and disgust of some; the devouring gaze of others; and the interested inspection of whomever cared to inspect." Such attire on public streets was considered to be "a startling sight to the uninitiated," and the Honolulu Advertiser conjectured that either the South Pacific or Africa "would probably have to be visited to find virtuous women so scantily clad, making such exhibition of their persons in public." In 1918, the matronly 'lanai lizards' of the Outrigger Canoe Club Woman's Auxiliary agitated for a law to stop such a "promenade of nymphs in the semi-nude", and finally the 1921 Territorial Legislature passed the Desha Act, prohibiting persons older than fourteen to traverse any road or highway in the City and County of Honolulu in a bathing suit, "unless covered suitably by an outer garment reaching at least to the knees". This law was not repealed until 1949.

The Draining of Waikīkī

In the gardens at ʻĀinahau: The wetland agricultural ponds were not the only landscape features affected by the dredging of the Ala Wai Canal. The waterways in Kapiʻolani Park that surrounded Makee Island also disappeared, as did the picturesque grounds at ʻĀinahau.

Looking upstream from the mouth of Kuʻekaunahi stream (right). Prior to the building of the Ala Wai Canal, this rivulet emptied into the ocean at a point near the intersection of ʻŌhua and Kalākaua avenues.

*D*uring the opening decades of the twentieth century, the development of Fort DeRussy and the construction of numerous hotels and prestigious residences brought substantial changes to Waikīkī. Despite these changes, however, much remained the same. Most of the area either 'Ewa of Lewers Street or mauka of

Ponds behind Waikīkī, circa 1886.

Kalākaua Avenue (approximately 85% of modern Waikīkī) remained under water. This property was used as duck or fish ponds, and for the cultivation of rice and taro. These well established agricultural and aquacultural systems continued to exist side by side with the more urban, resort oriented aspirations of Waikīkī until the 1920s when the wetlands were eliminated.

The wetland agricultural systems in Waikīkī were reputedly built during the reign of Kalamakua (circa 1400) and were a major source of taro and fish for pre-contact Oʻahu. The introduction of Western diseases decimated the native Hawaiian

Diamond Head from Waikīkī Road. Many of the taro fields in this area survived until after World War II.

population and, as a result, many taro *lo'i* (fields) and *loko* (fishponds) fell into disrepair by the 1830s and 1840s. Wetland agriculture was revitalized during the 1860s and 1870s, when former sugar plantation workers of Chinese and later Japanese ancestry leased the lands to grow rice and raise *'ama'ama* (mullet) and *awa* (milk fish). By 1890 these endeavors, as well as the cultivation of taro and the raising of ducks, were well established in Waikīkī, existing on the fringes and in the shadow of the beach's recreation-oriented community which was becoming more and more pronounced.

Waikīkī duck pond circa 1915. The pursuits of wetland farmers on occasion conflicted with that of the emerging visitor industry, as in February 1913, when Chinese, who needed to drain their 'rice patches' along 'Āpuakēhau stream for harvesting, dug a trench through Waikīkī beach causing the waters of the Outrigger Canoe Club's lagoon to empty into the ocean. Muck from the opened lagoon 'smeared' the sea and drove away a considerable number of bathers, some of whom filed complaints with the Hawaii Promotion Committee requesting "that something be done to prevent a future display of river sweepings in what has been advertised as one of the most romantic and perfect temperatured bathing places in the world."

The waters which made Waikīkī's agricultural system possible derived from three major streams. These streams—the Pi'inaio, 'Āpuakēhau, and Ku'ekaunahi—drained Makiki, Mānoa and Pālolo valleys, and gave rise to the occasional reference to Waikīkī as 'Waikolu' [three waters]. The Pi'inaio emptied at the present site of Fort DeRussy, the 'Āpuakehau between today's Royal Hawaiian and Moana hotels, and the Ku'ekaunahi near Kapahulu Avenue.

Agitation for the reclamation of Waikīkī's wetlands began in 1906 with a thirty-six page report by Lucius Eugene Pinkham, the president of the Territorial Board of Health. Pinkham's report declared Waikīkī's "swamps" to be "deleterious to the public health", a breeding ground for mosquitoes. It recommended that a "lagoon" be constructed around Waikīkī to divert the stream water from the district. No action was taken on Pinkham's report. During 1909–1910, however, the U.S. Army reclaimed part of Fort DeRussy, and in 1911 realtor Percy Pond purchased an 8.06 acre fishpond, Loko Ka'ōhai, had it filled, then subdivided and sold it as the Beach Walk Tract.

In 1913 Pinkham was appointed territorial governor and the movement to reclaim Waikīkī began to take shape. The Department of Public Works studied the new governor's earlier proposal in earnest and, in 1918, the legislature appropriated $100,000 for the excavation of the drainage canal. During the next two years the 161 acres in the canal's 800-foot wide right of way was procured, and in December 1920 the contract to build the canal was let to the Hawaiian Dredging Company.

Work on this relatively straightforward construction project began in 1921. During the initial phase of work the fill gathered from the ocean at the mouth of the canal was pumped overland to build up the site where McKinley High School now stands.

The Ala Wai Canal under construction. In the background is Kalākaua Avenue with its West Indian mahogany trees that were planted in the twelve-foot central 'parking', or boulevard, in 1912. At the time the avenue was described as an eighty foot-wide "glaring expanse of dust". The Department of Public Works believed the 'parking' would reduce the road's upkeep by $1,000/annum, but some citizens opposed the measure fearing the trees would block the views of Diamond Head and Punchbowl.

The dredge in operation. With the completion of the canal, the tax office increased the assessed value of Waikīkī lands by 800%.

In 1925 the City Planning Commission requested the citizens of Honolulu to submit suitable Hawaiian names for the renaming of the Waikīkī Drainage canal. From the twelve names received, the Commission felt that Ala Wai [waterway], the name suggested by Jennie Wilson was the "most euphonic". Other entries included: Aloha Channel, Ka Wai Lanamalie [peaceful floating waters] Manoloa [long channel], Wailana [smooth water] and Lokoiʻa Muliwai [fishpond stream]. An engineer with the Planning Commission was quick to note that, "the fact that Mrs. Wilson is the mayor's wife had nothing to do with the choice of the name."

Jennie Wilson in 1893, when she performed at the Chicago World's Fair. The identity of her companion is not known.

Lucius E. Pinkham: Father of the Ala Wai

Governor Pinkham handing the keys of office over to Charles McCarthy, at 'Iolani Palace. In the foreground stands Secretary of the Interior Franklin K. Lane.

Lucius E. Pinkham

*L*ucius E. Pinkham was the prime mover for the construction of the Ala Wai Canal, and might be considered the man ultimately responsible for the transformation of Waikīkī into an urban area. In 1905, when president of the Territorial Board of Health, he prepared a plan to 'reclaim' the wetlands of Waikīkī. Like so many plans, this one was shelved. However, nine years later the former head of the Board of Health had the incredible opportunity to implement his plan, when President Woodrow Wilson appointed him governor of Hawai'i.

Born in Massachusetts in 1850, Pinkham, while in high school, injured his leg while taking a horse over a jump, and as a result was unable to walk or work between the ages of 19 and 22. The leg injury, which would bother Pinkham throughout life, precluded his going to college, and influenced his decision to remain a bachelor.

After recovering from this injury, Pinkham worked in the grain and coal industries in the Midwest. In 1891 he came to Hawai'i to erect a coal handling plant for the O'ahu Railway and Land Company, a job which took three years to complete. In 1898, he returned to Hawai'i, again to serve Dillingham interests as a cashier for Pacific Hardware Company. He became manager of this Dillingham subsidiary, and then on 13 April 1904, was appointed president of the Territorial Board of Health. Concluding his term of office in 1909, Pinkham again departed Hawai'i, but in 1913, on the recommendation of California Congressman William Kent, President Woodrow Wilson submitted his name to the U.S. Senate as the fourth governor of Hawai'i. The Senate's confirmation was heavily contested both in Washington and Hawai'i, as people claimed he was neither a resident of the Islands nor a Democratic party regular.

Wilson's supporters, however, stood firm and on 30 December 1913, the new governor arrived in Hawai'i. Much of the energy of Pinkham's four-year term was devoted to putting in motion the plans and appropriations needed to implement his earlier Waikīkī Reclamation Plan. The efforts of his administration eventually resulted in the construction of the Ala Wai Canal.

As governor, Pinkham was outspoken, honest to a fault, and a man of high ideals. As a result his public career was "often stormy and almost always moving in an atmosphere of controversy." Upon his retirement from government, Pinkham returned to the US in a vain attempt to restore his flagging health. Here, near penniless, Pinkham passed away on 2 November 1922, the first of Hawaii's Territorial governors to die.

A 1903 view of Waikīkī from the roof garden of the Moana Hotel—prior to the construction of the Ala Wai Canal.

Waikīkī in 1936—after the canal was completed.

Fishing on the Ala Wai Canal.

Subsequent fill was employed to eliminate the ponds and low lying areas adjacent to the new canal. By 1924, the canal had been completed as specified; however, it was widened an additional 100 feet in order to satisfy the need for more inexpensive fill to complete the reclamation of the mauka lands in portions of the McCully tract. With the filling of the underwater sectors of Fort DeRussy in 1928, the entire project was officially completed.

In a matter of eight years, the work of countless anonymous Hawaiians, work that had survived for centuries, was undone. The construction of the three mile long, 250 foot wide, 10–25 foot deep Alā Waī Drainage Canal radically altered the face of the area. Its former landscape largely obliterated, Waikīkī embarked on a new period of growth. The shape that this growth eventually would take was inconceivable in 1928, but one thing was certain, the area's destiny was to be an urban one.

Waikīkī and the Ala Wai Canal, circa 1930. The curved canal in the center of the photograph is the terminus of Mānoa stream.

The Grand New Waikīkī

The Royal Hawaiian Hotel under construction; the main drive in 1926.

Work Along Main Drive.

With the opening of the Royal Hawaiian Hotel on 1 February 1927, Waikīkī entered a select circle reserved for resorts of worldwide distinction. By offering magnificent hotel accommodations as well as a splendid climate and beautiful natural setting, the already famous beach cordially and genuinely extended its 'aloha' to travelers of the highest class.

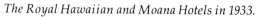

The 'pink palace' towered over its neighbors and had a majestic aura new to Waikīkī. Sheer massiveness, capped by a central tower that soared 150 feet above the street, enabled the Royal Hawaiian to join the Moana in dominating the beach's palm-filled skyline. Furthermore, its four hundred rooms, each with a bath, balcony, and view of either mountains or ocean, almost doubled the guest capacity of Waikīkī.

The Royal Hawaiian from the present site of the Sheraton-Waikīkī Hotel.

The doorman at the Royal Hawaiian opens the door of a 1932/1933 Packard for a guest. During the 1920s the average stay in Hawai'i was four to six weeks. Visitors either rented cars for $50/week ($125 with driver), or brought their own vehicles with them at a cost of $60/ton.

The new hotel also redefined the meaning of elegance for the district. Its 1929 rate of $14/night, American plan, readily attested to this. In comparison, the Moana charged only $8/night for similar services, and both the Halekūlani and Niumalu asked a mere $5/night. At the Waikīkī Inn a visitor could stay, without meals, for $1.50/night.

Tea time at the Royal was a more formal affair than at its predecessor, the Seaside.

The 'gallery', a lounging area in the Royal Hawaiian Hotel.

In addition to grand rooms and meals, the Royal Hawaiian also offered its guests the use of an auditorium with two stages, a ballroom, a motion picture theater, and a banquet hall. Designed by the New York architectural firm Warren & Wetmore, whose reputation was established by such works as New York City's Ritz-Carlton, Biltmore,

The ballroom of the Royal Hawaiian. The ceiling beams were painted by Guiseppe Gentiluomo of New York. His designs were also painted on the walls and ceilings of the gallery, which the Honolulu Advertiser *described as a "fairyland of bird and plant life drawn from the artist's imagination".*

Belmont, Vanderbilt, Commodore, Chatham and Ambassador hotels, the Broadmoor in Colorado Springs, as well as a number of Atlantic City hostelries, the hotel was world class, and the only one in the Islands truly capable of handling conventions.

The hotel's showcase grounds encompassed approximately fifteen acres, most of which are occupied today by the Sheraton-Waikīkī Hotel and the Royal Hawaiian Shopping Center. Laid out by the nationally renowned landscape architect R.T. Stevens of Santa Barbara, California, this park-like setting contained over forty varieties of trees and shrubs that presented "a network of beauty unsurpassed". The tall coconut trees of the ancient Helumoa grove set the dominant tone for this botanical display, and numerous pathways allowed people to wander amidst lush tropical foliage. Along with these immediate grounds, the hotel also developed and maintained the Waiʻalae golf course for patrons more athletically inclined.

The Royal Hawaiian beach boys. Duke Kahanamoku kneels in the center of the group.

*The six-story center section with its campanile rose 150 feet above the street, making the
hotel the tallest privately-owned building in the Territory. In order to accommodate such
a grand scale, the County Board of Supervisors in September 1925 amended Honolulu's
building ordinance to raise the legal height limit from 75 to 150 feet. The amendment
passed against the advice of the City Planning Commission.
City Planning Engineer Charles R. Walsh, declared:*

*The [Planning] Commission does not believe that sky scrapers are consistent with the
typical Hawaiian beauty we are so anxious to conserve.*
*We preach and in all our descriptive literature elaborately state that Honolulu is dif-
ferent than our American cities, yet we are rapidly becoming the same kind of city as
every other American urban center. All our unusual and strictly Hawaiian aspects
are being absorbed into typical American dollar producing enterprises. Wherever the
difference of a few dollars is concerned for the benefit of business development over
what we term our natural beauties, there is no longer any argument as to which features will be favored. . . . There is no doubt that the management of tall hotels and
office buildings can be somewhat more efficient than on lower structures of the same
floor space. But efficiency of private enterprises carried to the point of public detriment should not be permitted.*

The building of such a superb hotel, the cost of which ran in the neighborhood of
five million dollars, reflected the confident light in which a growing number of people
viewed the prospects of the tourist industry in Hawai'i generally and Waikīkī
specifically. These people believed that the efforts to promote the Islands as a visitor
destination, which were initiated by the Hawai'i Promotion Committee in 1903 and
continued by the Hawai'i Tourist Bureau, were finally about to reap unprecedented
rewards.

Other projects, such as the Aloha Tower and the passenger ship *Mālolo*, also bespoke
this optimistic belief. In 1921 the territorial government commenced the
modernization of its docking facilities. These efforts included the construction of the
nine-story Aloha Tower, the tallest building in Hawai'i at the time. Four years later, in
1925, the Territorial Hotel Company, a subsidiary of Castle & Cooke, began plans for
the Royal Hawaiian Hotel, and in the same year the Matson Navigation Company,
another subsidiary of Castle & Cooke, issued a $7.5 million dollar contract for the
Mālolo, a 650 passenger luxury liner. This ship, the first built by Matson to transport
primarily people, had more cabins with private baths than any ship in the world and,
when completed, was the fastest vessel on the Pacific. Capable of traveling 22 knots
(25mph), the *Mālolo* cut two days off the former 6½ day voyage to Hawai'i from the
West Coast. With projects such as these and the completion of the Ala Wai Canal,
Waikīkī appeared to be on the verge of a dynamic and prosperous future.

Keeping pace with the expectations engendered by the opening of the Royal
Hawaiian and the completion of other undertakings, the owners of Waikīkī's principal
cottage style hotels upgraded their facilities. Between 1926 and 1931, major building

The Niumalu Hotel stood on the lands now occupied by the Hilton Hawaiian Village.

programs were undertaken at the Pierpoint, Halekūlani and Waikīkī Inn. This new construction was all architect designed and substantially contributed to a new and more urban atmosphere in Waikīkī. No longer a retreat from downtown, the beach forsook the days of 'home spun' boarding house charm and simplicity and consciously sought to embody, in a contemporary and cosmopolitan fashion, the essence of Hawai'i with its allure for the tourist.

The Heen Investment Company led the way in the improvement of Waikīkī's hotel facilities when in May 1926, it purchased the Pierpoint Hotel and its neighbors, Hummel's Court and Cressaty's Court. The company refurbished and relandscaped this cluster of cottages and its six acres of grounds, renaming it the Niumalu [Sheltering Palms]. They also built a number of new structures, thereby increasing the hotel's capacity to 125 guests. A new main building, with its dining room and dance floor, became the focus of the complex. Designed by architect Afong Heen, this large frame building featured a steep 'Hawaiian', or double-pitched hip, roof, a porte cochere supported by lava rock columns, and an open interior with a courtyard in the center. The hotel well represented the emerging 'Hawaiian style' of architecture. It was one of the earliest commercial buildings in Honolulu to be rendered in this style and, in the words of hotel manager Edward C. Lubbe, the Niumalu's architecture and plantings were "an effort toward the last word in Hawaiian atmosphere as the tourist would want it. It comes as near to a grass hut with a girl in a grass skirt dancing the hula as one can get."

The lobby of the Niumalu presented guests with a very open outdoor space with large, arched portals and a courtyard.

The courtyard featured a 'musical rock fountain' with a speaker system hidden within the central rock garden. The dining room is seen on the far side of the courtyard.

The enclosed rear lānai provided for elegant lounging.

The Halekūlani Hotel's main building was completed in 1931.

The expansion of the Halekūlani Hotel also was designed with the Hawaiian style of architecture in mind. In 1926, hotel owner Clifford Kimball commissioned C.W. Dickey, the local architect most frequently associated with the Hawaiian style of architecture, to design three cottages for the grounds recently acquired from A.M. Brown. Subsequently, the hotel built several larger cottages along similar lines, and in

The Waikīkī Inn after it was remodeled in 1928. The hotel remained in operation, under a variety of names, until 1960, when it and the Steiner residence were removed as part of the Kūhiō Beach improvement project.

1929 the hotel's main building, the former Robert Lewers residence, was demolished. Its replacement, completed in 1931, also followed Dickey's plans and was considered one of the finest examples of architecture to capture the Hawaiian feeling. The *Honolulu Advertiser* stated that the new hotel was truly "kamaʻāina" in spirit and accurately reflected the "personality of the land." For years to come this complex set a romantic ideal for Hawaiian architectural design in Waikīkī.

Rather than build in a Hawaiian style, the owners of the Waikīkī Inn opted to reconstruct their premises in the "old Norman" style, which would "lend age to the structure and make it appear of that early English period when the word 'tavern' was in vogue". Architect Louis Davis provided the plans for the 1928 remodeling of the Waikīkī Inn which increased the number of rooms at the hotel to 104 and included space for eight shops. Such diverse commercial activities as Benson Smith Company's drug store, a beauty salon, a branch of American Sanitary Laundry, the barbershop of Edwin T. Miller, Thayer Piano (which advertised ukuleles for sale), Ben Seelig's bathing suit shop, Theodore T. Drega's curio and shell emporium, and Tanaka's florist studio occupied these new stores. Like all the improvements of the period, these mercantile ventures intended to better service the anticipated rush of tourists to Waikīkī. The presence of such activities in the district indicated that the beach had come of age, and the *Honolulu Advertiser* noted, "Guests of the hotel and others living in the neighborhood will no longer need to go downtown for so many of their wants. Business has moved out to them."

Unfortunately the boom in the tourist trade did not appear immediately. Travelers to Hawaiʻi steadily increased throughout the 1920s, with 1928 signaling the first year since the mid-nineteenth century whaling period that over 20,000 people visited the Islands. However, the crash of the stock market on 29 October 1929, led to a significant decline in vacationers arriving in the Territory. By 1932 the number of visitors had dropped to 10,400 and it was not until 1935 that predepression figures again began to be equalled. Waikīkī's hotel industry, which by now boasted fifty percent of Hawaii's hotel rooms, struggled through this period which frequently saw occupancy rates lower than thirty percent. No major new hotels were built along or near the beach until after World War II, although several more modest operations, such as the Pua-Lei-Lani Hotel, did open in the middle 1930s. However, the Royal Hawaiian reigned supreme as the Islands' largest hotel until 1955 when the Princess Kaʻiulani opened its doors.

The completion of the Ala Wai Canal not only gave impetus to the development of Waikīkī as Hawaiʻi's primary visitor destination, but also expanded the district's potential for residential use. During the period 1913–1927, the demand for housing in Honolulu grew along with the city's population. To accommodate these needs, large

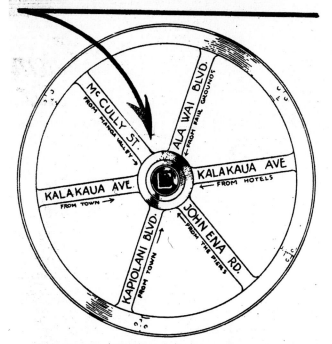

Percy Pond and the Subdivision of Waikīkī

*R*ealtor Percy Pond was among the earliest people to recognize the potential of converting Waikīkī's fishponds into profitable land, and as such was one of the prominent figures in the residential development of Waikīkī.

Born in Ohio on 2 February 1870, Pond was an Oberlin College graduate, who came to Hawai'i in 1896 to be a *luna* at 'Ewa Plantation. The following year he joined Castle & Cooke, and two years later, in 1899, became bookkeeper and clerk for the S.N. Castle Estate. In 1900 he launched his real estate career when McClellon & Pond handled the opening of the College Hills Tract in Mānoa. He remained active in real estate, and by 1939 the *Honolulu Star Bulletin*, with only slight exaggeration, claimed that if Pond, "didn't have something to do with the sale of your home, then he likely subdivided the property."

Pond's involvement with Waikīkī began in 1911, when he purchased the Loko Ka'ōhai fish pond, as well as a parcel on Diamond Head. He took land from the latter to fill the former, which he subdivided as the Beach Walk tract. The six acre fishpond cost $3,250, or 1.5¢/square foot, to acquire, and when filled the subdivision lots sold for 10¢ to 15¢/square foot. By 1927, land in this area was valued at approximately $2/square foot. Other Waikīkī projects in which Pond was involved included the purchase and sale of the Royal Grove Tract in 1915, and the promotion and sale of Dewey Court (1915) and 'Āinahau (1919).

A vigorous, enterprising man, Pond involved himself in a variety of business ventures besides real estate. He operated Pond Dairy in Kapahulu (1904-1914); started Kemoo Farm in Wahiawā (1914), and formed an automobile sales agency (1918), which eventually became Pond Company. He also was active in many community organizations, including the Honolulu Ad Club, where he was chairman of the committee for the preservation and marking of historic landmarks. In this capacity he compiled and financed the publication of *The Kamehameha Highway*, a booklet that told legends and stories associated with various points of interest throughout the Islands.

His concern for Hawai'i's heritage was also demonstrated during the sale of 'Āinahau, when he was instrumental in having the Wilder Estate deed Ka'iulani's banyan to the Daughters of Hawai'i as a park. For many years the Daughters of Hawai'i maintained this beloved tree and its 2,400 square foot lot. During World War II J. Donovan Flint cared for the premises and in November 1948 purchased it from the Daughters. Residents of Tusitala Street, led by Charles J. Brenham, had complained in March 1948 that "rats, cats, red berries, leaves by the thousands, dead branches and bird droppings have made this tree a first class nuisance", and claimed it was a detriment to the homes in the area, five of which were located under its spreading boughs. With the property in private ownership the neighbors renewed their pressure to have it removed, and in February 1949, Flint acquiesced to their

Ka'iulani's banyan tree, which Pond was instrumental in preserving in 1919.

The extension of Lili'uokalani Avenue in 1924 opened another new Waikīkī subdivision.

demands, and had this flourishing tree, "one of the city's main tourist attractions", taken down. Four years after the banyan's demise none of the thirteen residents who initially had protested the presence of the tree lived in Waikīkī, and only two couples remained in Honolulu.

*Walter Gustlin's idyllic realty advertisement of 1926
contrasted sharply with others of the time.*

estates and former agricultural/pasture lands in Waikīkī, as well as Makiki, Mānoa and Kaimukī, were transformed into residential tracts.

In Waikīkī, between 1913 and 1921, the large *kama'āina* landholdings virtually disappeared. With the subdivision of Queen Lili'uokalani's property, Hamohamo, in December 1913, the former haunts of royalty began to yield to the real estate market's demand for moderately priced house lots. In February 1915 the trend continued, when Prince Kalaniana'ole sold a six-acre portion of King Kalākaua and Queen Kapi'olani's Waikīkī estate to Percy Pond for $32,500. Pond, who had previously been involved in the development of the Beach Walk Tract, immediately converted these grounds into the Royal Grove Subdivision, complete with coconut-tree-lined streets, concrete sidewalks, and both gas and water lines. Priced between $925 and $1,500, with one third cash down and the balance, plus 7% interest, due in three years, the ninety 5,000 square foot lots moved briskly.

The success of the Royal Grove Tract encouraged further subdivision activity. With the conclusion of World War I in 1919, Prince Kūhiō sold the remaining portion of Kalākaua's former estate, which became the Pualeilani Tract. Contemporaneously, eleven and two-thirds acres of Archibald Cleghorn's former estate, 'Āinahau, were placed on the market with lots selling for $3,500 and up. These sold quickly and before the end of the year over one hundred new residential units were built in Waikīkī. More activity followed, when parcels in Diamond Head Terrace, the former estates of James Campbell and George Beckley, were offered to prospective buyers in 1921. With this subdivision the last of the large, readily-developable landholdings in Waikīkī had been broken up. Further residential development had to wait for the draining of the area by the Ala Wai Canal.

The first post-canal residential ventures, the McCarthy and Bigelow Subdivisions, were owned and bore the names of the Territory's governor and the Superintendent of Public Works, respectively. They opened in 1925, and Kalākaua Acres and Moana Estates followed in 1926 and 1927. These subdivisions had to compete with the contemporaneous marketing of St. Louis Heights, Wilhelmina Rise, Maunalani Heights, Kamehameha Heights, and the Nu'uanu Dowsett Tract, as well as new sections opening in Kaimukī, Makiki and Mānoa. Construction on the Waikīkī sites was slow and primarily modest in character.

The *Honolulu Advertiser* noted the changes resulting from the subdividing of Waikīkī lands, and commented that, "the old romantic days of the royal entertainments where the island belles and beaux and the officers of ships of many nations danced, are being thrust farther back in memory and a new romance, which though it dates back to the time when the first man built his first house, is ever new, crowds in to take the place of the memories of other days." This new romance of home ownership, however, was not to be, as most new housing in Waikīkī was for rental rather than owner occupancy. Visitors from around the world took up transient residence in the district, as did numerous local people who worked in support of the growing tourist trade.

The colonial style residence of Paul Carter, designed by Mark Potter in 1934, was one of the imposing dwellings erected along Ala Wai Boulevard.

An aerial view of Waikīkī in 1933. Many of the recently created residential lots between Kalākaua Avenue and the Ala Wai Canal sit vacant. The tall spire in Makiki belongs to Central Union Church.

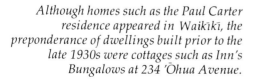

Although homes such as the Paul Carter residence appeared in Waikīkī, the preponderance of dwellings built prior to the late 1930s were cottages such as Inn's Bungalows at 234 'Ōhua Avenue.

Where the Action Was

With its hotels serving as magnets to draw people to the area, Waikīkī gradually developed into a hub of social activity. It offered leisure time amusements beyond that of the surf and beach scenes. Zoning ordinances passed by the City Supervisors in 1927 concentrated Waikīkī's commercial activity onto Kalākaua Avenue, further encouraging the transformation of the road from a sedate thoroughfare to a center of glamorous activity.

One of the first enterprises to recognize the expanded commercial potential of Waikīkī was the Aloha Amusement Park Company, which was directed and owned by

In 1924 the Aloha Amusement Park changed its name to Waikīkī Park. The arcaded entry was modeled after the Palace of Fine Arts Arcade at the San Francisco Exposition of 1915. Designed by Honolulu architects Ripley, Davis and Fishbourne, it was an attempt to further lend credibility to the developers' claims that they were working for the betterment of Honolulu.

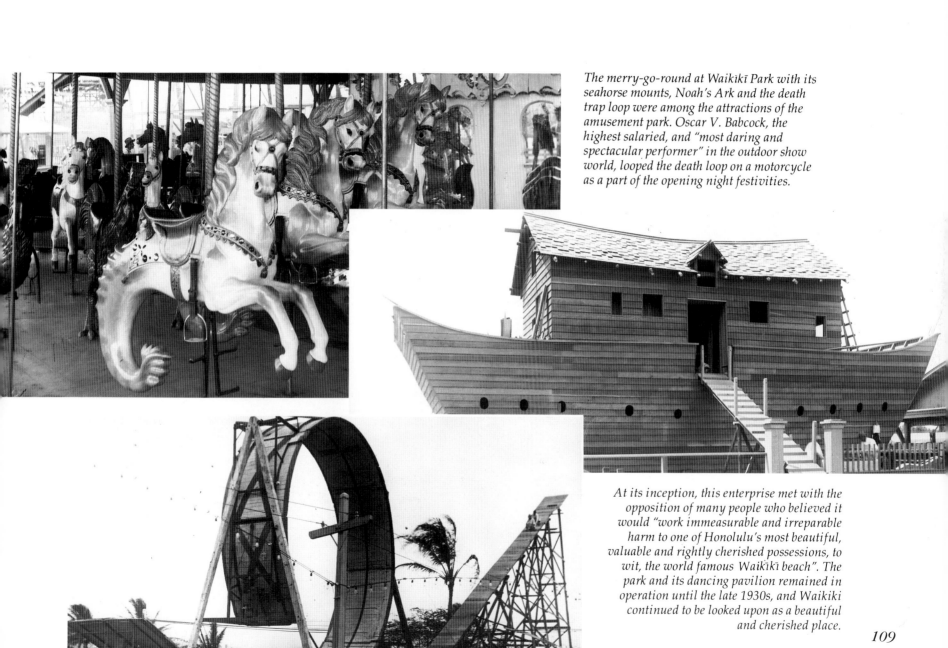

The merry-go-round at Waikīkī Park with its seahorse mounts, Noah's Ark and the death trap loop were among the attractions of the amusement park. Oscar V. Babcock, the highest salaried, and "most daring and spectacular performer" in the outdoor show world, looped the death loop on a motorcycle as a part of the opening night festivities.

At its inception, this enterprise met with the opposition of many people who believed it would "work immeasurable and irreparable harm to one of Honolulu's most beautiful, valuable and rightly cherished possessions, to wit, the world famous Waikīkī beach". The park and its dancing pavilion remained in operation until the late 1930s, and Waikiki continued to be looked upon as a beautiful and cherished place.

109

Saturday night fireworks at the Territorial Fair Grounds, as viewed from across the Ala Wai Canal. The fairgrounds were situated on the lands now occupied by the Ala Wai golf course. The Territory purchased the property in 1918, prior to the construction of the Ala Wai Canal. In 1921 the governor conveyed these lands to the Territorial Fair Commission, which constructed a seven hole golf course on the property as one of its attractions. In 1938 the golf course was expanded to its current size, the first eighteen hole public golf course in the Territory.

110

such people as George P. Cooke, Alfred Castle, W.H. McInerny, F.D. Lowrey, and James D. Dole. Located on the five-acre Hobron property which was bounded by John 'Ena Road, Kālia Road, Fort DeRussy and the residential lots fronting on Kalākaua Avenue, the land had to be drained and filled prior to construction at a cost of over a quarter of a million dollars. When completed, the Aloha Amusement Park contained such attractions as the 'Big Dipper', the 'Aerial Swing', 'dodgem' cars, a merry-go-round, and the largest outdoor dancing pavilion in the Islands, not to mention a midway with games, a penny arcade with 110 machines, and two acres of planted gardens.

The *Honolulu Advertiser* extolled the opening of the amusement park and noted that it brought "life, excitement and bustle" to an area "where only four short months ago only the dismal croak of a bull frog in the swamp broke the stillness of the peaceful night atmosphere." The newspaper went on to claim that the completion of the park added "another laurel to the wreath of Honolulu's progressiveness and one of which she should be justly proud."

The *Advertiser*'s accolades stood in sharp contrast to the strong objections that had been voiced by numerous people less than five months earlier. Various sectors of the

The Beach Barber Shop stood at 2844 Kalākaua Avenue.

The Banzai Cleaning Shop, operated by Tokuji Harakawa, was bedecked with flowers on the completion of its new building in 1935, on Kalākaua Avenue, at the present site of the Hawaiian Regent Hotel. Established before World War I, it served Waikīkī clientele for more than thirty years.

The Kapiʻolani Clothes Cleaners and the N. Aoki General Merchandise Store and Gasoline Station date from 1913, and were located on Kalākaua Avenue and Paoakalani Street. Much of the Aoki's business derived from home deliveries outside the Waikīkī area. Their delivery van is parked in front of the store. Although the store is now gone, the Aoki Mini Mart remains in Waikīkī, at 2080 Kalakaua Avenue.

community, most notably the Outdoor Circle and nearly all the residents of Waikīkī, felt that the amusement park idea would not be in keeping with the character or image of Waikīkī. They deplored the visual impact which would be made by the 'park' ("a sadly misleading term") and also criticized the placement of such an "atrocious ballyhoo bazaar" in the midst of a tranquil residential district. In their eyes, no site existed in the entire city where such structures as a Ferris wheel or an elevated 'scenic' railway "would be so glaringly incongruous and 'out of the picture' as in Waikīkī".

Despite such objections, the Aloha Amusement Park commenced operations on September 14, 1922. During the first two hours after the gates were flung open an estimated 10,000 people, including the governor and mayor, flocked through the turnstiles. With the opening of the park, the word 'entertainment' took on a new meaning for Waikīkī: a meaning that included catering to the masses.

Other entrepreneurs also saw the commercial possibilities for Waikīkī. During the late 1920s and 1930s a number of shops designed to meet the needs of the tourist emerged along Kalākaua Avenue. They ranged in function from drug stores and beauty parlors to boutiques and curio shops. The most enduring and perhaps most

endearing of these was the Honolulu branch of S.&G. Gump Company of San Francisco. Opening in February 1929, it presented tourists and residents alike with a handsomely appointed atmosphere filled with ancient and modern *objet d'art*, the 'heirlooms of mankind'. The store communicated an aura of class, and provided customers with high quality goods, as well as a sense that Waikīkī was indeed bringing the world to Hawai'i's doorstep.

Gumps, 'a treasure house in the Pacific', operated for over twenty-two years under the management of Alice Spalding Bowen, the woman responsible for bringing the store to Hawai'i. Designed by architect Hart Wood, the building and its merchandise were a blend of oriental and western themes. In 1951, Gumps was forced to close, the proceeds of its liquidation going to the settlement of the A. Livingston Gump estate.

114

Helen Kimball's Oriental Shop was one of the many short-lived ventures offering 'curios'. These souvenirs allowed visitors to ascertain that Hawai'i was 'real', and indeed, teeming with exotic merchandise as well as exotic sights.

Elmer Lee's Grass Shack, 'Hale Pili', was located between the Royal Hawaiian Hotel and the Outrigger Canoe Club. During the late 1930s this colorful shop offered visitors ukuleles, surf boards, coral, 'Waikīkī Willie' sharkskin swim togs, and 'Grass Shack' colored silk shirts, as well as drinks of coconut milk and pineapple juice.

Have You Visited Helen Kimball's
ORIENTAL SHOP
Look for "The Red Lacquer Temple Shop"
ON LEWERS ROAD—NEAR ALL BEACH HOTELS

115

Annie's Lei Stand opened on the grounds of the Royal Hawaiian Hotel in 1928. The proprietor's daughter still operates Lili's Lei and Flower Shop in the Royal Hawaiian Shopping Center.

During the 1920s and 1930s, Manuel K. Richards, a pioneer taxi operator, ran a taxi and tour guide service at the corner of Kalākaua and Ka'iulani Avenues. He chauffered residents and visitors alike, with the former Queen Lili'uokalani being among his early clientele.

Lau Yee Chai as viewed from Kūhiō Avenue. In 1966 the building was demolished to make way for the Ambassador Hotel.

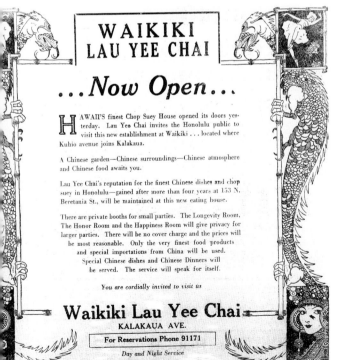

Along with the shops, restaurants also began to dot Kalākaua Avenue. For most of the 1920s, the Waikīkī Tavern was the only place other than hotel dining rooms where a person could obtain a meal. By the end of the decade, however, other restaurants, such as the Barbecue Inn, the Fuji Tea House, and the Savoy Grill were on the scene. Like the small shops, most of the 1930s eateries came and went. The only establishments with sufficient durability to become landmarks were the Barbecue Inn and Lau Yee Chai Chinese Restaurant, and a trio of drive-in restaurants (the K.D.I.

Opening on 21 December 1929, under the proprietorship of P.Y. Chong, Lau Yee Chai was described as an "elaborate and ornate chop suey house", and "the world's largest and most beautiful Chinese restaurant".

117

The sign at Kau Kau Korner, originally located on the present site of Coco's Coffee House, was a tourist 'must'. The postcard of this sign was the number two seller for Kodak during the 1930s; only a view of Diamond Head sold better.

[Kapi'olani Drive-Inn], Kau Kau Korner, and the K.C. Drive-In with its waffle hot dogs). Catering to the young, the drive-ins became the end-of-the-evening haunts for teenagers out on dates or nights on the town.

The Kapi'olani Drive-Inn started as a concession in Kapi'olani Park. In 1951 owner Francis James Tom moved his business to the corner of Ala Moana Boulevard and 'Ena Road, where it is best remembered for its neon hula girl sign and fifteen cent hamburgers.

The K.C. Drive-Inn, located at the corner of Kalākaua Avenue and Ala Wai Boulevard, was one of the earliest drive-ins in Hawai'i, opening in 1926.

The Green Lantern, at the corner of Kalākaua Avenue and Uluniu Street, was one of a number of restaurants that thrived in Waikīkī during the mid-1930s.

The Waikīkī Theater opened on 20 August 1936, with the showing of **Under Two Flags** starring Claudette Colbert, Ronald Colman, and Rosalind Russell in a "story of flaming love and smoldering rebellion." The premier movie palace in Hawai'i, its C.W. Dickey design celebrated the beauty of both Hawai'i and current architectural trends. The theatre's interior decor placed the audience in a verdant papier-mache landscape of Hawaiian flora, the work of Homer Merrill. A rainbow and palm trees framed the screen; banana trees, lauhala, papaya, night blooming cereus and other local plants adorned the walls; and hand-painted hibiscus in relief decorated the aisles.

New attractions such as the Waikīkī Theater, built in 1936, and the 1940 Waikīkī Bowl featuring ten lanes in a 'semi-outdoor' environment, also drew funseekers. The music of the Johnny Noble band, the Waikīkī Stonewall Quartet, Don McDiarmid's South Seas Orchestra, Ted Dawson's Waikīkī Lau Yee Chai Rainbow Rhythm Band, and the Harry Owens Band further enhanced the area's flourishing night life, and by 1938 the *Honolulu Advertiser* could state without exaggeration, "What was once just another street is today a thoroughfare of life and gaiety. The lights may be dimmed in other sections of Honolulu—they may be even turned off—but not along Kalākaua Avenue."

One of the two hula dancer murals by Marguerite Blasingame, which graced the lobby.

121

Harry Owens: Mister Hawai'i

Hawai'i exerted a profound influence on Harry Owens, and in turn, he made an indelible mark upon its music scene. Through his music and media presence, Owens put Waikīkī and Hawai'i into the minds of millions, or, as Bob Hope noted, "Mention tradewinds singing in the branches of a coco palm and I think of Harry Owens. Mention tropic moonlight, rippling waters, a million stars and steel guitars—again, Harry Owens. Speak of lovely, brown-skinned, hula maidens and I think of . . . Well, enough of that! What I mean is the guy is Mister Hawaii."

Born in O'Neill, Nebraska in 1902, Owens began playing cornet in a school band when he was nine. By 1926 he had his own band, which toured the western states until May 1934, when Owens accepted the position of musical director at the Royal Hawaiian Hotel.

Upon his arrival in Hawai'i, Owens became enchanted, if not infatuated with the Islands, and for the next thirty years his bands were known for the Hawaiian music they played. Owens essentially extended the *hapa haole* sound introduced by Sonny Cunha and Johnny Noble. He made the steel guitar an integral part of his

Harry Owens was associated through much of his career with the music of the Islands, which he did so much to popularize.

122

Harry Owens on the beach at Waikīkī with his daughter, Leilani, the namesake of his 'Sweet Leilani'. Bing Crosby's hit recording of this tune remained on the 'Hit Parade' charts for twenty-eight consecutive weeks—a record that has never been equalled.

Johnny Noble and the original Moana Hotel Orchestra, 1918. Owens succeeded Noble as music director at the Royal Hawaiian in 1934.

arrangements, and he injected into the Island music, "a new sweetness of melody, a new appealing rhythm, [and] an enchanting soft charm."

His musical style is best exemplified in 'Sweet Leilani', which he wrote on 20 October 1934, the day after his daughter, Leilani, was born. Bing Crosby recorded the song in 1935, and it became an overnight hit, selling more than a million records in a few weeks. Crosby also sang the song in the movie *Waikīkī Wedding*, and it won an Oscar for the best film song of 1937, making it the first song not written expressly for a movie to earn such recognition.

The success of 'Sweet Leilani', coupled with the radio program 'Hawaii Calls', which Webley Edwards and Harry Owens inaugurated on 14 October 1935, with Owens composing the theme song, resulted in a Hawai'i craze in the US. Capitalizing on this fad, Harry Owens and his Royal Hawaiians went to California in December 1937 to play at the Beverly Wilshire Hotel, then appeared in several films including *Cocoanut Grove*, for which Owens scored the music. After an engagement at the Royal Hawaiian Hotel in 1940, the band again returned to California with Owens' latest discovery, Hilo Hattie; and Owens scored the music for the movie *Song of the Islands*.

In October 1949, a new door opened as CBS televised Owens' band live from the Aragon Ballroom in Santa Monica, California. This marked the start of what would be a weekly television program, sponsored by United Airlines for many years. Initially, this Hawaiian music show played only in California, but by 1954 its popularity led CBS to expand its broadcast area to include Nevada, Arizona, Alaska and Hawai'i. In July 1958, Harry Owens and his trumpet bade TV farewell, but he continued to tour with his band until 1963, when he retired.

123

Screen star Charlie Chaplin, a frequent
visitor to the Islands in earlier years, passed
through Honolulu on 26 February 1936, and
had lunch at Lau Yee Chai with playwright
George Bernard Shaw, who also happened to
be in town. Honolulu novelist Shirland Quin
is seated with the famous pair. Chaplin had
just completed Modern Times, and was en
route to Indochina with his leading lady,
Paulette Goddard. The menu was vegetarian
in deference to Shaw's tastes.

The eight-year-old Shirley Temple caused an
uproar when she and her family vacationed in
Hawai'i in 1935. Over ten thousand fans
greeted her at the pier and on 5 August 1935,
she was made an official member of the
Waikīkī Beach Patrol.

By 1938 the Honolulu Advertiser claimed Waikīkī had made the "transition from a once rural community into a smart center, visited and enjoyed by the great and near great of the world".

Babe Ruth and Connie Mack were two of the members of the America League All Star team that visited Hawai'i in October 1934, as part of a two month exhibition tour of the Orient. The professionals defeated Hawai'i's All-Star team 8-1, on 25 December 1934, with Lou Gehrig blasting the game's only home run.

126   *'America's Sweetheart', Mary Pickford and her husband, musician Charles 'Buddy' Rogers, honeymooned in Hawai'i in 1937. The famous actress had previously visited Hawai'i in 1929, when she and then husband Douglas Fairbanks reigned as king and queen of Hollywood.*

Hollywood stars Carole Lombard and William Powell honeymooned at the Royal Hawaiian Hotel in July 1931.

Adriana Caselotti, the voice of Walt Disney's Snow White.

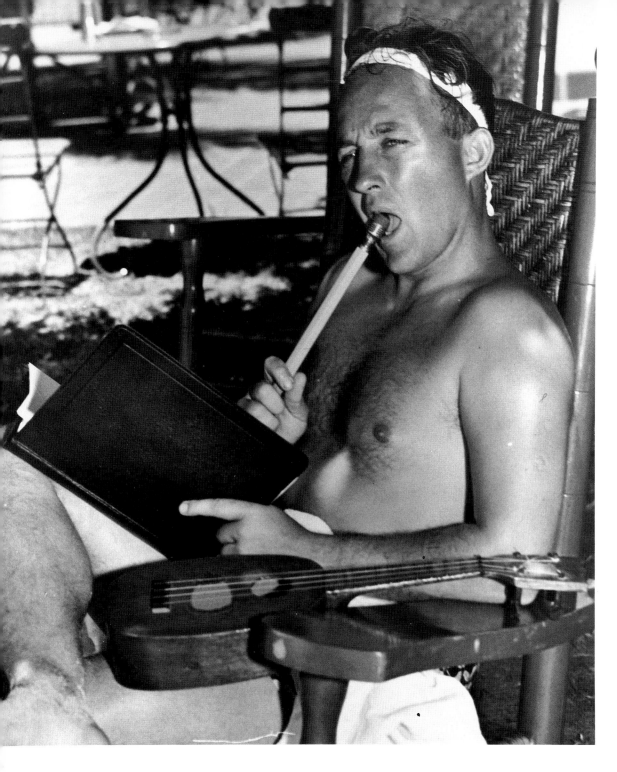

Bing Crosby stayed at the Royal Hawaiian Hotel in 1935, to rest and gain inspiration for his forthcoming film, Waikīkī Wedding.

"Some may have called it [Waikīkī] glamorous then. All admit that it is glamorous today. Not so much the scenery. Not so much the coral sands and the velvety surf. But the people who frequent the sands and the surf and the hotel grounds."

Groucho Marx and his wife Ruth vacationed in Hawai'i for three weeks in 1936, following the completion of the Marx Brothers' comedy, A Day at the Races.

On 3 November 1934, child actor Peter Lawford at the Royal Hawaiian with his parents, Sir Sidney and Lady Lawford.

In the midst of this dazzling new world, George Mossman and his family introduced Lālani Village. Located on the grounds of the former Lemon estate near Kapi'olani Park, Lālani Village attempted to preserve and perpetuate in a viable economic context, the language, culture, traditions, and lore of Hawaii. Developed during a time referred to as a 'Hawaiian renaissance', the village was an outgrowth of

Lālani Village introduced visitors to Hawaiian crafts, music and life style.

The presence of Kuluwaimaka, the former court chanter for King Kalākaua, lent the village much credibility.

Pualani Mossman teaches a hula to Vicki Baum, author of Grand Hotel.

George Mossman's daughters—Pi'ilani, Leilani, and Pualani—danced at the village.

a Hawaiian school project which Mossman had started in 1928. Students were charged tuition and visitors paid admission to enter the village. There they learned about the traditional style of Hawaiian life and enjoyed entertainment. Opening on 19 May 1932, the village was a popular Waikīkī attraction until the start of World War II, when the arrival of tourists, the village's main source of income, drastically declined and led to the closing of the project.

131

Wartime Waikīkī
by Dan Boylan

*T*he war revolutionized the Islands' economy. Throughout the 1930s tensions grew between the United States and Japan. As the possibility of war increased between the two Pacific powers, Hawai'i's strategic military position was enhanced. The attack on Pearl Harbor doubled the Territory's population to over a million, half of whom were soldiers, sailors, marines and civilian war workers.

Waikīkī did not escape the influx of military. For four years it offered its hotel rooms to servicemen. Soldiers tramped the hotels' hallways, dropped ashes on their carpets, swilled booze in their saloons, and diminished their refinement with the atmosphere (and aroma) of a barracks.

With the peace, Waikīkī's hotel owners thought their major problem lay in chipping off camouflage paint and refurbishing their establishments to their pre-war splendor. But the war never ended. It became, instead, the uneasy peace between communist and capitalist worlds which would continue to lend importance to Hawai'i's strategic location. Twice during the twenty years following VJ day communists and American capitalists would meet in open warfare: Both times in Asia. Hawai'i would remain a leading producer of sugar and pineapple, but it would also remain an armed camp. Hundreds of thousands of servicemen would continue to serve part of their tours in Hawai'i's military installations.

They would come to know the Islands' sunshine, their beaches, and their warmth, both climatic and human. They would take their memories home with them: to New York and Chicago, to Kalamazoo and Keokuk.

Staff Sergeant Joe DiMaggio, along with thousands of other GIs, saw Hawai'i while in his nation's service. The Yankee Clipper was one of several professional ball players assigned to bolster the 7th Air Force's baseball team. He remained in the Islands for about sixty days during the summer of 1944. He was second in the Hawai'i Baseball League in batting with an average of .421 and 5 home runs. Like many servicemen, Joe DiMaggio returned to Hawai'i after the war, visiting here after the 1949 World Series.

The barbed wire enclosed beach at the Royal Hawaiian during World War II. The Royal Hawaiian and other prime Waikīkī properties, including the former Steiner residence, were used as clubs for the military personnel stationed in the Islands.

Waikīkī Takes Off: Tourism in the 1950s
by Dan Boylan

The view from the Rosalei Apartments in 1955 when the Royal Hawaiian, Moana, Surfrider, Waikīkī Biltmore, and Princess Ka'iulani dominated the skyline.

*I*n 1959 the Board of Directors of Matson Navigation Company agreed to the sale of four Waikīkī Hotels, the Royal Hawaiian, the Moana, the Princess Ka'iulani and the Surfrider, for $17.65 million. To be sure the hotels occupied prime pieces of Waikīkī real estate; but they were proving costly and cumbersome to operate. Matson saw itself primarily as a shipping company, and the corporate treasury needed cash.

Matson's hotel sale stands as the greatest gaffe in Hawai'i's corporate history. Within a half-dozen years of Matson's hotel divestiture, the growth of Hawai'i's visitor industry would transform a Waikīkī hotel into a veritable money making machine, and turn each square foot of Waikīkī real estate into a gold nugget.

134

The twelve-story Rosalei Apartment Building was the first high-rise apartment constructed in Hawai'i. Opening on 10 March 1955, it offered prospective residents a choice of 21 studio and 132 one bedroom apartments. The building's name is a loose Hawaiianization of local singer and school teacher Rosaline A. Stephenson's first name.

Yet in 1959 Matson's directors could make a solid case for their decision to sell. In the fourteen years since the end of World War II they had watched tourism grow at a slow and measured pace. Many spoke of its potential, but few saw its explosion into the Islands' single largest industry. That would have required economic, political, and technological vision beyond the ability of Matson's most far-sighted director.

The Islands' charms enjoyed more than the word of mouth publicity of returned servicemen. Hawai'i became a product thrust into a mass, national market-place. In 1950 the Hawai'i Visitor's Bureau spent half a million dollars promoting the Territory's attractions. Fifteen years later it spent three times as much.

The drive for statehood augmented these visitor industry expenditures. Each post-war congressional session included debate on a Hawai'i statehood bill. The

Designed by Gardner Dailey, the eleven story Princess Ka'iulani Hotel (as seen in these three photos) was the tallest building in Waikīkī when it opened its doors on on Kamehameha Day, 11 June 1955. This "beautiful and brilliantly modern resort hotel" attempted to capture "the spirit of Hawai'i".

The Kāhili Room & Bar featured a koa bar with inlaid Mother of Pearl. Murals by Esther Bruton Gilman presented a stylized pageant of South Pacific migrations to Hawai'i and the evolution of the kāhili.

debate spilled over into the nation's news and editorial columns as well. Statehood's opponents, of course, did little for the Islands' image, but Statehood's proponents were in the majority. They wrote not only of Hawai'i's readiness to enter the Union, but of an economically sound, very American, mid-Pacific community.

The presence of Hawai'i in the American consciousness was further strengthed by Arthur Godfrey. Every Wednesday night, throughout the 1950s, he strummed his ukulele and sang (off-key) Hawai'i's praises to the newly emerging television audience. A former Schofield Barracks soldier, James Jones, did his part to spread Hawai'i's fame. In 1951 his novel, *From Here to Eternity*, led the best seller lists. The 1954 movie version won an academy award and created in the public imagination the possibility of moonlight grappling, *à la* Burt Lancaster and Deborah Kerr, on Hawai'i's

Geometric designs, inspired by ancient Hawaiian game shields, decorated the hotel's elevator doors.

A Japanese teahouse, an "almost exact duplicate" of a summer house at Katsura Palace in Kyoto, was a focal point of the pool and garden area.

A view of Diamond Head from the corner of Nāmāhana and Kūhiō Avenues in 1959, as compared with the similar view today.

A last look at Diamond Head from Kalākaua Avenue. The Foster Tower, completed in 1962, was the first building to mar the pedestrian's view of the famous peak. The twenty-five story Holiday Inn, under construction in the background, would obliterate any impression of the landmark from the street. When completed in 1970, the 650 room Holiday Inn was the largest hotel building in Waikīkī, as well as in the entire Holiday Inn chain.

Lewers Street and Kālia Road, circa 1958. On the left is the seven-story Edgewater Hotel, the tallest building in Waikīkī until the advent of the Biltmore.

Roy Kelley: The Wizard of Waikīkī

Newlyweds Roy and Estelle Kelley arrived in Honolulu on 13 September 1929 with $106 in their pockets. They rented a cottage in Waikīkī, and in 1932 built their own home and the six-unit Monterey Apartments at Seaside and Kūhiō Avenues. Thirty-one years later, in 1963, the newspapers referred to Kelley as the 'Wizard of Waikīkī', the largest hotel developer and owner in the state, with approximately 2200 rooms under his control. By building an empire of moderately priced hotels he made Waikīkī an affordable place for the middle income visitor.

Upon graduating from the University of Southern California's school of architecture in 1927, Kelley worked briefly in California before coming to Hawai'i as chief designer for Honolulu architect C.W. Dickey. For nine years Kelley worked in Dickey's office, eventually becoming an associate. In December 1938, he established his own firm, which specialized in designing apartment houses.

Besides doing apartments for his clients, Kelley also developed several Waikīkī properties of his own. During 1939-1940 he expanded the Monterey Apartments, and in 1941 he constructed the twelve unit Town House Apartments. At the conclusion of World War II, the Edgewater Beach apartments were acquired by Kelley, and in 1945 the thirty-six room main building of the Islander Hotel was completed on Seaside Avenue, the first post-war hotel project in Waikīkī.

The next two years saw Kelley build the Ala Wai Terrace with its 192 apartments, and the 100 unit Edgewater Hotel at Lewers and Kalia Road, the first major hotel to be erected in Waikīkī since the completion of the Halekūlani in 1931. A second 100 room section of the Edgewater was built in 1950, and in 1955 the ten-story, 350 unit, Reef Hotel burst upon the scene. With the opening of this new beachfront hotel, the *Honolulu Advertiser* stretched its imagination to its wildest limits and speculated that perhaps someday Waikīkī might be able to support a 700 room hotel, to which Kelley responded, "Anything can happen in Waikīkī."

Between 1955 and 1973 Kelley built such hotels as the Reef Tower, Reef Lanais, Waikīkī Surf, Waikīkī Surf East and West, Outrigger, Outriggers East and West, Coral Reef, Waikīkī Tower, and Waikīkī Village. All of these were designed as non-luxury hotels with rates at the bargain basement level (for example, in 1963 a single room in a Kelley hotel ran between $8.50 and $12/night as compared to a Waikīkī average of $20/night). These prices spoke for themselves, for without the aid of advertising or a large mainland booking agency Kelley's hotels have enjoyed higher than usual occupancy rates, which for most years bordered on close to 100%.

Kelley officially retired in early 1974, however, he remains actively engaged in the affairs of Hotel Operating Company of Hawai'i, Ltd., the firm he established to handle his properties. He serves as the company's chairman of the board, with his son, Richard, as president. This firm manages 6,500 rooms in their twenty Waikīkī hotels, which include the Prince Kūhiō and the recently completed Seaside Surf.

In 1955, Kelley told reporters, "I have had implicit and abiding faith in Waikīkī since the day I landed in the Islands in 1929, and I see no reason to change my thinking. In fact I have put all my eggs in one Waikīkī basket and will put more in as the future warrants."

The Islander Hotel, which once stood on Seaside Avenue, was the first Waikīkī hotel built following World War II.

Roy Kelley and his wife, Estelle.

141

beaches. In 1961 Elvis Presley starred in a popular culture classic, *Blue Hawaii*, and thus wed his considerable appeal to that of the Islands.

Advertising agencies, statehood publicity, and the entertainment industry contributed greatly to the development of a mass tourist market for Hawai'i. But a major technological breakthrough was required: Regular passenger jet service from the mainland.

Prior to World War II, ocean liners brought the bulk of visitors to Waikīkī's beaches. It took up to a week to sail from Los Angeles or San Francisco to Honolulu. Add to that the train or airplane trip to the west coast, and a visitor to Hawai'i needed at least a month's vacation. Such an extensive holiday, coupled with the cost of passage guaranteed that Waikīkī's beaches belonged to the rich and well born.

The arrival of Pan American Airways' China Clipper in 1935 presaged the dramatic changes of the post-war era. In 1935 it took an airplane from the west coast 18 hours to reach Hawai'i; twenty years later the flight still took 12 hours. The Islands remained a long way away. However, when Pan American inaugurated Boeing 707 service to Hawai'i on 6 September 1959, the once tiring and, to some, frightening twelve to fifteen hour trip suddenly became a five-hour lark.

For Hawai'i, 1959 was pivotal. Not only was jet service introduced, but on 14 August 1959 President Dwight Eisenhower signed the Hawai'i Statehood Bill into law, certifying the nation's approval of the Islands' Americanness. Statehood subtly changed Hawai'i's image in the tourist market, a change which immeasurably broadened its appeal. Hawai'i might be lovely brown-skinned maidens, exotic nights, and strange Polynesian food, but it was also hamburgers, hot showers and American soil.

The Waikīkī Branch of Bishop Bank (left) and the McInerny clothing store (below) were built in 1951 and 1953 respectively. Designed by Vladimir Ossipoff of the architectural firm of Wimberly & Cook, both buildings were demolished in 1977 to make way for the Royal Hawaiian Shopping Center.

Waikīkī was on the verge of inundation by a massive wave of visitors. Statistics tell the story. Prior to World War II, Hawai'i's overnight visitor count never rose above 30,000. By the mid-1950s it hovered around the 100,000 mark. In 1958 it was 171,588; in 1959, the year of Statehood, jets and James Michener's *Hawaii*, it jumped to a quarter million. Five years later it doubled to half a million, and it has continued to escalate reaching four million in 1980, and four and one half million by 1984.

In order to accommodate this tremendous influx in people, Hawai'i's visitor industry grew, with Waikīkī as the center of activity. Starting in the mid-fifties with the efforts of Matson, Roy Kelley, Henry Kaiser and others, Waikīkī developed rapidly. For much of the 1960s and 1970s the construction crane became part of the district's skyline, and the kik-boom, kik-boom, kik-boom of pile drivers in search of solid ground became the rhythm to which inhabitants choreographed their day. Waikīkī's appearance underwent a dramatic transformation, the results of which are before us today.

Credited with the definite purpose of attracting visitors who enjoyed the romantic, the Hawaiian Village epitomized that thrust of 1950s Waikīkī which stressed Hawai'i's lush and exotic setting.

The entry to the Hawaiian Village's main building featured aluminum louvres covered with abaca cloth. These served as wind control baffles.

Henry J. Kaiser and Fritz Burns purchased the Niumalu Hotel and its surrounding lots in 1954-55 and commissioned architects Welton Beckett and Ed Bauer, and landscape architect Richard Tongg to design the Hawaiian Village Hotel, a "South Sea paradise that visitors expect ...and Islanders appreciate". This complex of twenty-four thatch roofed guest cottages, "turned away from the tower-of-glass architecture to establish a setting and atmosphere indigenous to the Islands."

The guest cottages lay adjacent to one of three swimming pools. The pools were all below sea level and contained continuous flowing, filtered ocean water.

The Barefoot Bar at the Hawaiian Village, with its lauhala lined walls and ceiling, became a familiar site to television viewers who tuned into Hawaiian Eye.

Today

Waikīkī Today

Although Waikīkī is included within the sprawling city limits of Honolulu, the Ala Wai Canal separates it from the rest of the city and makes it appear as a metropolis unto itself. Approximately 285 of its 450 acres are privately owned.

From at least the 1850s people viewed Waikīkī primarily as a recreational area. The lure of its sandy shore consistently attracted both local and foreign visitors seeking leisure and a change in scene. Recognized as a special place, serving a special function, it nevertheless maintained a sense of common experience and continuity with the greater community of Honolulu. However, during the last twenty-five years the explosion in the visitor industry has propelled the area away from the city's larger communal psyche making modern Waikīkī a distinct entity unto itself. An urban resort, it has become separated from the rest of Honolulu in a way much more profound than the visual demarcation conveyed by the Ala Wai canal.

Rather than address the needs of Honolulu's community, the district's chief end is to embody and glorify the two major images of Hawai'i: a modern, up-beat urban resort, and an exotic 'South Seas' paradise. These two images are the underlying premises on which modern Waikīkī has been built, and it is in their light that the district should be considered. The area is an urban resort with a romantic tropic soul, molding its environment and energy to meet the needs and idyllic visions of its clientele.

Filled with tourists and other fleeting figures, Waikīkī primarily responds to the dreams, expectations, and requirements of a transitory population. About seventy percent of the approximately 62,000 people, who on a normal evening find shelter in the area, are visitors to Hawai'i. They stay on O'ahu an average of 5.77 days before disappearing to other shores. The remaining thirty percent of the population—the 17,000 residents of the district—is also distinguished by a rather transient, non-local character.

The majority of Waikīkī's so-called 'permanent population' (81%) were born outside Hawai'i, and 72% of them have resided in their present dwelling for less than five years. A large segment of these people are single (63%), and they live almost exclusively in high-rise apartments, with 98% of the district's housing units located in buildings with five or more apartments, and 72% in buildings with fifty or more units. The district's racial mixture of 64% Caucasian and 30% Oriental or Pacific Islander, more than reverses corresponding figures for Honolulu (33% Caucasian and 59% Oriental or Pacific Islander). Thus while millions of people throughout the world equate Waikīkī with Hawai'i, Island residents do not share this view. For them, Waikīkī is a 'different place', an anomaly, when compared to Honolulu or anywhere else in the world. One step removed from traditional time and space, the district's purpose and people distinguish it from the normal routine of life.

The golden crescent of sand and bodies which people travel around the world to see and become a part of.

149

Waikīkī is people passing through, but moving slow.

The pulse of Waikīkī is based on this everchanging populace composed of apartment and hotel dwellers, plus the hundreds of Island residents who flock to Kalākaua Avenue for an evening's entertainment or the beach scene. Such transience holds the potential for instability. However, the powerful image of Waikīkī as a glamorous, vacation oriented, urban space in the midst of a tropical paradise is a strong bond which gives coherence and definition to the district, and which allows the transient faces to congeal into a stereotypical Waikīkī crowd: short haired servicemen; Japanese honeymooners; middle aged couples rotund with material success; sunburned, upper middle class teens; glad hand conventioneers; grass peddling pedicab operators; high gloss hookers; Island residents celebrating some special occasion, or just out for a dinner/movie; and costumed youths in skimpy attire or grass skirts handing out leaflets and selling all sorts of bargains. They stream through the streets and flesh out Waikīkī for the flash of the moment. Eternal, their show goes on around the clock. Given a storyline based on visitor expectations and a backdrop composed of the built environment and commercial infrastructures, new actors regularly fill the cast-of-thousands roles and bring life to the district.

A Krishna incarnation of Waikīkī seeks your wealth in the name of spiritual health.

A pedicab confab.

151

This passing population requires no specific history to support its identity. Its traditions are grounded in the expectations of a change of scene, and its mores derive from a sense of being one step removed from daily life. The majority of these people have discovered the fifth freedom—freedom of vacation: the extraction of self from life's responsible routines, including work, community, and whatever other cares they left at home. Their laid back attitude and the phantasmagoric garb in which they clad themselves proclaims their liberation, whether they are strolling down the Avenue in their matching aloha wear, abbreviated swimsuits, gingham dresses, or the latest new

Waikīkī is people seeking a break from life.

wave fashions. The crowd's vitality, exhilaration, and diverse declarations of freedom from social constraints generate the exuberant energy and slightly-out-of-sync character that is Waikīkī. The people make the scene, and their attitudes, like their status, reflect the here and now. For them, Waikīkī is a transient experience, a fleeting temporal moment, or, to use Wordsworth's words:

> . . . *a phantom of delight*
> *A lovely apparition, sent*
> *To be a moment's ornament.*

The fifth freedom: the freedom of vacation.

Waikīkī is the beach and the life that surrounds it. Joe Maize, Waikīkī's sand-castlist-in-residence made the sand sculpture.

But above all, Waikīkī is a beautiful tropic isle.

The courtyard of the Hawaiian Regent Hotel.

The entry portico and gardens at the Royal Hawaiian Hotel.

Waikīkī's energy and transitory tendency is exhibited not only in its population, but also in its built environment. In comparison to the ruins of Rome, the pyramids of Egypt, or the gardens and temples of Kyoto, the eternal verity that draws people to Waikīkī is a romantic vision of a tropical paradise here on earth. Upon this image Waikīkī has been built. Sustained by the beach, ocean, sun, and human imagination, as well as advertising, this idyllic conception requires no precise, readily identifiable buildings to elicit a concrete image in peoples' minds. Diamond Head more than adequately says it all; and a walk in its shadow epitomizes the Hawai'i experience for the visitor.

The Hilton Hawaiian lagoon. Diamond Head and, even more immediately, the Rainbow Tower frame this seaside Shangri-La.

The Waikīkī Trade Center, the work of architect Warner Boone, was completed in 1980. Twenty-two stories of slimline design, its smart, stylish, well-appointed spaces proclaim a classy, with-it sense of now that epitomizes the contemporary look of Waikīkī.

The fanciful, exuberant ice cream parlor, Evviva Gelato, was designed by Honolulu architect Stanley K.S. Chun.

One of many elaborate embellishments contributing to the overall effect of the Waikīkī Trade Center, these second level stained glass windows were crafted by Gangwer Design Studio.

The posh, neon illuminated Galleria shopping mall features such shops as Abbraccio, C'Est La Vie, Magique, Silks Honolulu and Celine.

Designed by Maxwell Stackman of Beverly Hills, California, the mall moves easily from the street and beautifully flows through the first floor of the Trade Center where plastic strands of twinkling electric lights are suspended in space to bedazzle star-struck eyes.

The Grape Escape, a chic, casual sidewalk cafe next to a fountain of cascading elegance, further enhances the amiable luxuriance of the Galleria.

However, this world famous beach is not only a laid back tropical place, but also an enclave of perceived pleasures/diversions of that most miraculous of moments: NOW. Waikīkī reverberates with the presence of today. Bold, sleek high rises such as Discovery Bay or the Waikīkī Trade Center, and innumerable chrome and mirrored interior spaces flash the slick gloss of the late 1970s/early 1980s. Appealing to the immediacy of their day, these designs place Waikīkī in the mainstream of contemporary excitement and action. They fulfill one of Waikīkī's major promises by providing a chic, upbeat metropolis offering glamour galore. This fashionable urban resort image has been a major thrust of the district since at least 1962, when *Paradise of the Pacific* recognized that if Hawai'i was to compete in the international tourist market, visitors would have to be shown, *"why Hawaii is a better point-of-call than Miami, Las Vegas and Cannes, . . . not why it is as good as Tahiti."*

The Waikīkī Biltmore hotel hosted many memorable moments, but none was more memorable than its demolition, which happened a little after eight AM on 28 May 1974. Three hundred pounds of TNT wired in a series of 236 mini-explosions was used to blow up the building before a crowd of thousands. After detonation, the twelve story, 200,000 ton building wavered for a minute and thirty-seven seconds before it came tumbling down. Thus the tallest building in the Territory in 1955 became a pile of rubble nineteen years later, a major metaphor bespeaking Waikīkī's transient character. Or as the mainland demolition expert David Martin put it, "[it's the] newest thing we've taken down. You just don't see a 1955 coming down."

The argot of the neon named shave ice concession in the Royal Hawaiian Center, and the lavishness of the koa-galore Discovery Bay McDonalds all bespeak the dazzle of the modern Waikīkī scene. Geoffrey G. Paterson & Associates was responsible for the Big Mac's interior design, which when completed in 1978, had the most expensive McDonalds' interior in the world.

As paeans to the present, the current architectural 'masterpieces' are but the most recent in a succession of buildings that have partially enabled a fifty square block area to compete with the magic and pizzazz of major urban centers around the globe. A number of these once modern showpieces—the Waikīkī Biltmore Hotel, McInerny's store, and the Royal Theater—have already fallen to the wrecker's ball, indicating the temporal climate which envelops Waikīkī's built environment.

The fourteen-story Waikīkī Circle Hotel at 2464 Kalākaua Avenue dates from 1963.

162

More recent buildings have made the Ala Wai Apartment Hotel at 2319 Ala Wai Boulevard a mass of glass with a view to nowhere. Built in 1953, this building was one of the earlier commissions of Wimberly & Cook.

Of those trendy projects of yesteryear that still stand, many appear outdated. Fading monuments from a time gone by, apartments such as the Fairway Villa, Ala Wai East and Ala Wai West, no longer glow with the hopes of the radiant city. Other quaint utopian visions of an earlier today, such as the Waikīkī Circle Hotel, the Ala Wai Apartments, the Ambassador Hotel, and the Tree House Apartments, border on becoming architectural curiosities of that long-ago era (by Waikīkī standards), the 1960s.

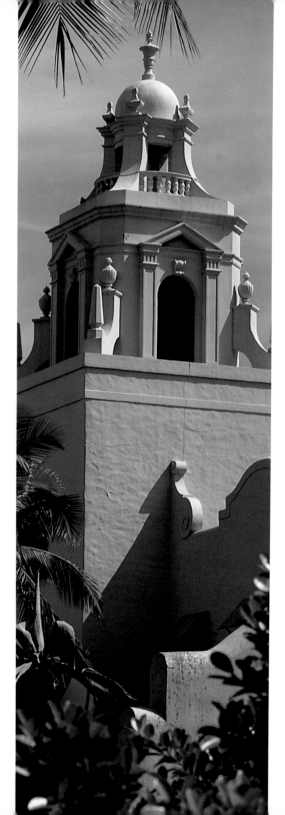

The Tree House Apartments at 337 Lewers, 'honestly' displays its structural support members as part of its facade. Designed by architect John Tatum in 1961, the building adhered to the modernist postulate, 'form follows function'.

The blue Pacific Ocean as viewed from a corridor leading from the Royal Hawaiian Hotel's lobby to the beach. The 'pink palace' is perhaps the only building in Waikīkī with sufficient history and prominence to stand as an image of the district.

163

The view from the top of the 'Ilikai elevator.

The first glass elevator in Hawai'i made its appearance in 1963, when architect John Graham incorporated it into the design of the 'Ilikai.

Less daring and in many respects more mundane designs, such as those of Foster Tower, the 'Ilikai, and the Reef Hotel, blend into the blur of sensory overload and passively occupy space in the streetscape. Although once described by the press in such glowing terms as "a bright episode in the colorful history of mushrooming Waikīkī", and "a great monument to Honolulu", they now stand disengaged from the high energy that adored all development. Stripped of that approving appeal, their newness long gone, their massiveness no longer a distinction, they now contribute little to the dynamics of the district.

In comparison with architectural proclamations of today, many of the technological 'innovations' which adorn Waikīkī buildings have a more eternal character. The glass elevator at the 'Ilikai, which its developers claimed would give ten views "that had never been seen before by man" for every one that the building eliminated, still imparts a momentary, forty-two-second, thrill. It and its counterpart at the Sheraton-Waikīkī continue to incite the imagination and instill a sense of the extraordinary.

Another technological toy, equally lasting, is the Top of Waikīkī, a revolving restaurant, built in 1965. An impressive technological trick, the experience of dining while rotating high above the ground was sprung on the world in 1933 at Chicago's

The thirty-one story Sheraton-Waikīkī Hotel with its glass elevator was completed in 1971. At the time of its opening, this 1,904 room hotel was the largest resort hotel in the world, and the fifth largest hotel in the world. The Kalākaua Avenue side of this triple winged, curvilinear building, designed by the architectural firm of Wimberly, Whisenand, Allison, Tong & Goo, focuses on the illuminated drama of the elevator.

The Top of Waikīkī revolving restaurant caps the Waikīkī Business Plaza, which was designed by Edwin Bauer in 1965. It was the second such revolutionary form to appear in Honolulu's culinary circle, with the Ala Moana Center's La Ronde (later renamed Windows of Hawai'i) opening four years earlier.

Century of Progress Exposition by industrial designer Norman Bel Geddes. Later, in 1962, the Seattle World's Fair also capitalized on this entrancing idea and reinforced the special midway atmosphere which befits the form. In recent years, additional bits of technological wizardry have continued the tradition of the new in the district. The six-story fountain in the middle of the Waikīkī Shopping Plaza, the Pacific Beach Hotel's 280,000-gallon indoor oceanarium (advertised as the world's largest), and Mitsukoshi's waterfall windows have attempted to further promulgate the sense of a special modern Waikīkī, replete with technological 'advances'. When compared to the earlier 'innovations', however, these more recent novelties are not as well integrated with their architecture. No longer incorporated into function, they appear contrived and garish. Whereas the purpose of the Top of Waikīkī and the glass elevators was to provide new vistas of paradise, the new engineering feats function in a more sculptural, 'look at me' manner. They do not capture the essence of technological progress for the betterment of humanity; instead they transparently serve as gimmicks to lure customers to shops and restaurants located around the superficial shows.

More than a mile of piping is required to circulate 10,000 gallons of water through the Waikīkī Shopping Plaza's multi-tiered fountain. The focal point of the Shopping Plaza, the six-story fountain is engulfed in a rampant clutter of signs, which, like the water show itself, strive to lure customers into the shops.

Mitsukoshi dominates the triangular parcel at the intersection of Kalākaua Avenue and Beach Walk, and draws a second look with its waterfall windows. Built in 1979, it was designed by Architects Hawai'i.

A practical, straightforward application of mechanical devices to accommodate a maximum of cars in a minimum of space, the Pro Park's eight-story stack garage, located adjacent to the Kūhiō Mall at 2301 Kūhiō Avenue, is a 'must see' for any technology buff.

Completed in 1972, King's Village stands at Ka'iulani and Koa Avenues. Designed by the San Francisco architectural firm of Moulton, Clark & Lawton, it employs the same ¾ scale as Disneyland.

Another Waikīkī fantasyscape, the Hilton Hawaiian Village's Rainbow Bazaar was designed by Leach, Cleveland & Associates of Los Angeles and Bauer, Mori & Lum of Honolulu. Within this architectural potpourri can be found an authentic Thai temple relocated from a rural village outside Bangkok, and a 400 year old Japanese farmhouse, which serves as the interior of Benihana restaurant. The bazaar opened in 1972, and seems more plausible than King's Village, thanks to its inclusion in a much larger, and equally incredible, resort destination complex.

Despite this shift in emphasis, the various examples of high tech gadgetry still impart a facade of 'tomorrowland' to Waikīkī. They skitter along the fringes of fantasy and fact, as does much of Waikīkī's clientele, and as such make superb icons in this realm of vacationland where the normal no longer applies. Areas such as King's Village, the shopping complex located at Ka'iulani and Koa Avenues, and the Rainbow Bazaar at the Hilton Hawaiian Village, stretch the fabric of reality to its outer limits and transport fantasy to the borders of absurdity. This is especially true of King's Village, a shopping complex outlandishly costumed in a pseudo-Victorian guise and plopped down incongruously in the middle of an urban sidewalk.

Completely unrelated to anything in Waikīkī or Honolulu, either past or present, and with its only apparent connection to royalty being the presence of a Burger King, the complex stands incongruously oblivious to its surroundings. Too out of place to be any fun, people hang out across the street to see if it will disappear along with their next puff of smoke.

The shops at the Hilton Hawaiian Village's Rainbow Bazaar, an architectural collage depicting Hawai'i's history and major ethnic groups, work somewhat better. Secluded on the western periphery of Waikīkī, separated from the strip by Fort DeRussy, they lie in an environment much more conducive to making someone

169

believe, that, yes indeed, this just might be 'anything can happen day'. Nestled along the drive between Buckminster Fuller's geodesic dome and the Rainbow Tower with its 26-foot-wide, 286-foot-high rainbow mural composed of 8,046 hand-painted tiles, each individually secured with a screw, and its oceanedge 'Pot o' Gold Lounge', the bazaar appears plausible. The excessive application of the rainbow theme makes the mind amenable to the fantastic. Although gauche, an air of subtlety still holds sway, making the bazaar less bizarre, almost normal within the context of tropic greenery

The Rainbow Tower is graced with Millard Sheets' tile rainbow mural, the tallest in the world when erected in 1968.

The lobby of the Sheraton-Waikīkī presents visitors with another larger-than-life image of paradise. Lois Taylor in her coverage of the opening of the hotel noted, "What the hotel somehow reminds one of is a beautiful, kind and obedient girl who somehow is 6 feet 3 inches and 185 pounds. Everything's there, but there's just too much of it."

The palm trees sway,
and the skies are not cloudy all day—
and of course, the ocean is there too.

The pool terrace at the
Sheraton-Waikīkī looks out
across the crowded surf scene.

and powerful architectural statements alluding to the natural beauty of paradise and the wonders of modern technology. The fantasy of fantasy becomes reality, and the mystique of Waikīkī is further enhanced.

Although prevalent and appropriate, modern and everyday fantastic realities are not the only faces of Waikīkī. The vibrant enchantment of the tropics itself towers above all the human made accretions. The built environment of today dissolves and becomes so much background 'noise' in the presence of endless summer. Profuse

The urban, highrise district is enveloped by open space: Kalākaua Avenue flows out into the greenery of Kapi'olani Park and the wide expanse of the beach/ocean, while the Ala Wai Boulevard and Canal offer further spatial releases from the high density of Waikīkī's commercial strip.

street plantings, a multitude of lānai, Diamond Head, and the everpresent ocean and beach confirm and reconfirm the fact that this place is indeed Waikīkī, the land of palm trees, surf, and sun. This is the essence that people from around the world come to enjoy.

This serene core provides a solid definition to an otherwise shimmering Waikīkī. The warm climate, lush vegetation, blue skies and tanned bodies make the romantic dream of Waikīkī as alive today as when Robert Louis Stevenson visited here. The natural environment establishes an identity and a sense of stability throughout the district. It is the area's dominant image, its eternal verity, despite the fact that many of its elements are but individual props in a swirl of changing scenes.

Only two blocks away from Kalākaua Avenue's intense energy, the Ala Wai Canal offers a respite of open space, tranquility and beauty.

The 39,000 square foot 'Lake Park Area' of the Waipuna condominium on 'Ena Road forms an oasis of lushness in an otherwise bustling section of Waikīkī. Built in 1971, the landscape was designed by George Walters. The forty-two story concrete 'megalith' reflected in the 'lake' is one of Discovery Bay's towers.

Waikīkī's world famous beach was originally a natural barrier beach that existed between the area's ponds and the ocean. The construction of seawalls along the ocean front in the early 1900s caused erosion problems so severe that by mid-century the beach was in danger of disappearing. Only the timely construction of groins and a periodic sand replenishment effort by the Army Corps of Engineers and others have allowed the beach to continue. Since 1939, much of the beach has been nourished by sands brought in by the truck and barge load from the north shores of O'ahu and the west shore of Moloka'i.

Similarly, the street greenery, which does so much to invoke a sense of the tropics, is another temporary prop. Consciously planted to fulfill a decorative function for an unnaturally short time span, a number of trees will have to be replaced well before maturing, when their roots and limbs encroach on the buildings, sidewalks, and streets they now adorn.

Such specifics, however, are of little consequence, other than to further confirm the temporal, yet timeless, character of Waikīkī. The area remains forever fresh and at the peak of life. Through constant change the romantic ideal is maintained and made real.

Waikīkī's full bloom of bright tropical splendor is perpetuated not only through its manufactured landscape, but also via the built environment. Whereas in the past Waikīkī hotels could boast of extensive grounds that were beautifully planted and contained picturesque cottages that intermingled with palms and hau trellises, the current $240 per-square-foot valuation on oceanfront Waikīkī property makes visions of landscaped grounds incredibly extravagant. The Royal Hawaiian's original fifteen acres of gardens has dwindled down to approximately six acres. Similarly, the grounds at the Hilton Hawaiian Village, the largest private landholding in the district, seem to be continually diminishing. In comparison, no other Waikīkī hotel can claim even this much open space surrounding its building.

174

Wimberly, Whisenand, Allison, Tong & Goo designed the 1,260 room Hyatt Regency Waikīkī with its two thirty-nine story octagonal towers. Waterfalls and an open-air lobby help define the courtyard.

An upper level promenade and bar provide vistas of the ocean. A simple, casual formality reigns supreme.

175

Christopher B. Hemmeter and the New Waikīkī

Hemmeter stands as one of the leading figures in Hawai'i's visitor industry, as well as one of the largest resort developers in the world. A man of decisive action, his Hawai'i projects embody a sensitivity that hopefully will point the way to the future for the state's tourism industry.

176

*I*n 1974 Chris Hemmeter ordered the demolition of the nineteen-year-old Waikīkī Biltmore Hotel. From the dust of that explosion arose a new vision of Waikīkī and tourism in Hawai'i, based on the premise that the tourist industry must consciously strive to make Waikīkī a high quality environment, attractive to visitors and residents alike. Hemmeter not only advocates such a position, but practices it as well, as his Hyatt Regency projects at Waikīkī, Waikōloa, and Kā'anapali demonstrate.

Born in Washington D.C. on 8 October 1939, Hemmeter grew up in Los Altos, California. Graduating from Cornell University in 1962 with a BS in hotel and restaurant administration, he came to Hawai'i, virtually penniless and $700 in debt. Shortly after arriving in Honolulu, he secured a position as assistant manager at the Royal Hawaiian Hotel. A year later, he and two partners formed International Innkeepers to construct and manage the food and beverage operations at the soon-to-open 'Ilikai Hotel. In 1965 Hemmeter sold his interest in this company, and with the profits started Associated Innkeepers, which developed and managed a number of restaurants in the International Market Place. In 1968 he sold these holdings for a reported $1.5 million.

A millionaire at 28, he next formed Hemmeter Investment Company which opened the Mark Christopher stores, selling clothing, jewelry and gifts, and eventually repurchased the International Market Place restaurants. Taking a giant step, the firm next invested $5 million to develop King's Alley, a 37,000 square foot shopping center, the design of which was inspired by the developer's conception of nineteenth century Honolulu. Built as an antidote to the perception that Waikīkī was becoming a "conglomerate of look-alike architecture", Hemmeter believed that the complex responded to Waikīkī's need for more lowrise development and a shopping area that was more formal than the International Market Place or Ala Moana Center.

Hemmeter's next move was his most dramatic, the construction of the $150 million, 1,260 room Hyatt Regency Waikīkī Hotel at Hemmeter Center, at that time the largest construction project ever undertaken in Hawai'i. The $75 million mortgage secured to pay off the hotel's construction loans, was the second largest single mortgage ever made on a hotel project in America, and the largest mortgage ever issued in Hawai'i. A loan of this magnitude requires payments of over $1,000 an hour on interest alone.

With the successful completion of this project, Hemmeter has moved beyond Waikīkī to develop the $250 million Hyatt Regency Maui, the $360 million Hyatt Regency Waikōloa on the island of Hawai'i, the $225 million Westin Maui hotel, and the $275 million Westin Kaua'i hotel. Concentrating on mega-resort developments, he recognizes that Hawai'i must strive for high quality hotel projects if the state is to maintain a competitive edge in the global tourist market.

Opening in 1976, the Hyatt's delightful passageways on the ground level floors press a joyful awareness of Hawai'i upon the pedestrian. The three ton sculpture hanging over the courtyard was executed by Edward M. Brownlee.

The 1,346 room Hawaiian Regent, opened in 1971, covers 5.3 acres and follows the plans originally conceived by architect John Tatum in collaboration with Chamberlain & Associates. Its use of lush courtyards, water, an open lobby, outdoor bars, lounges, and eating places, and a nicely landscaped upper level with a pool and tennis courts, pronounces a strong architectural statement on the beauty of Hawai'i.

The peaceful atmosphere of the outdoor Lobby Bar contrasts sharply with the buzz of activity adjacent to it in the lobby.

A bowered niche at the third floor pool.

Instead of relying on the presence of spacious grounds, a number of Waikīkī's better hotels capture a sense of the tropics through a flowing integration of their interiors and exteriors and judicious use of plantings. The lobbies of a large number of hotels, including the Hilton Hawaiian Village, Edgewater, and Hale Koa at Fort DeRussy, are for all intents and purposes outdoors, at one with the balmy tropic weather. This intimate relationship between architecture and the natural environment is also exemplified in the walk-through courtyards of the Hawaiian Regent and the Hyatt Regency hotels. Prudent juxtaposition of distinct quasi-interior/exterior spaces effectively conveys a sense of allowing the outdoors in. Well handled, these structures do not take either the indoors or the outdoors for granted, but make people conscious of the pleasant intermingling of the two.

The slick, open lobby of the Hale Koa Hotel at Fort DeRussy, and its entry. Lemmon, Freeth, Haines, Jones and Farrell were the architects of this stunning military hotel which opened in 1975.

The verdant poolside court of the Hawaiian King Hotel. Located at 417 Nohonani Street, this five-story building was constructed in 1962, following the plans of architect George K.C. Lee.

Similar sensations emanate from such diverse spaces as the Canlis Restaurant, the O'ahu Bar in the Sheraton-Waikīkī Hotel, the passageway to the Seagull Restaurant in the Kūhiō Village Resort Hotel, and the Jack-in-the Box located at the Waikīkī Grand Hotel on Kapahulu Avenue. These areas do more than capitalize on the benign climate; they dramatically glorify it. In comparison, other spaces, such as the lobbies of the Waikīkī Banyan, Island Colony, and Nāpualani hotels, and the International Market Place merely utilize, in a straightforward manner, the street as an extension of themselves.

Canlis' Restaurant at 2100 Kalākaua Avenue, designed by Wimberly & Cook in 1953, beautifully embodies the open, tropical style so appropriate for Hawai'i.   181

Small-scale, courtyard hotels offer a pleasant, hospitable atmosphere. Here paradise is virtually at your doorstep. The two-story Breakers Hotel at 250 Beach Walk offers a planted courtyard ambiance similar to the Hawaiian King, and rooms blending Japanese architectural motifs with conventional western forms. Immediately next-door to the Breakers, the 95 unit Hawaiiana Hotel presents a comparable setting; these two hotels were designed by Edwin Bauer in 1954 and 1955, respectively.

WE DEDICATE THIS ROOM
TO OUR GOOD FRIENDS
MR. & MRS. EARL McLAREN
The Breakers

The South Seas Village restaurant offers a typical tropical blend of indoor/outdoor dining.

Another intimate Waikīkī interlude is the Waikikian Hotel and Tahitian Lānai restaurant at 1811 Ala Moana Boulevard. The hotel's torch-lit garden lane, bordered by 84 units, leads to the Tahitian Lānai, where diners can enjoy dining in either private, single table abodes or larger pavilions, both of which are thatched roofed and open to the outdoors.

A number of smaller hotels—the Hawaiian Colony, White Sands, Breakers, and Hawaiiana—also nurture a special sense of Hawai'i's tropical beauty through their efficient utilization of the areas around their swimming pools to make verdant and intimate interior courtyards. The feeling of a casual, gardenlike Waikīkī, is further conveyed through such open air restaurants as the Tahitian Lānai, Banyan Gardens, and South Seas Village.

Sprawling out over a 34,275 square foot lot, the landscaped splendor of the Banyan Gardens offers a soft, intimate sense of dining in the tranquil twilight. The benign calm of this meandering space was conceptualized by the architectural firm Group 70 in 1983.

The main building of the former Halekūlani Hotel was integrated into Killingsworth & Associate's design for the 'new' Halekūlani, but the grand hau tree lānai has disappeared. The establishment emphasizes an open but extremely formal environment. Rather than heightening the Hawaiian experience for its guests, the Halekūlani sedately lays it out before them in a polished fashion.

In contrast to these restaurants and hotels, the Halekūlani Hotel, although open and sprawling, does little to heighten one's sense of Hawaiian paradise. With its understated elegance, it presents its guests with the essence of the Pacific: the ocean, the sky, and swaying palms. It accommodates the beauty of the Islands and makes it available, but does not glorify the romance of the tropics. No longer engendering the casual hospitality of the former cottage hotel, the Halekūlani, a peaceful escape from the world, could be located any place saturated with sunshine. An island unto itself, formal poshness reigns.

Waikīkī's built environment encapsulates the living legend of tropical paradise not only through the manipulation of space, but also through more graphic approaches. Applied ornamentation, such as that seen in the Jack-in-the-Box under the Hyatt Regency Hotel's parking facility, further broadcasts the message of Hawai'i. Ceiling fans circulating air-conditioned atmosphere, plastic 'stained glass' depictions of tropical flora and fauna, and Hawaiian landscape photographs on the walls, all contribute to reinforce the neon reminder over Jack's portal, 'Take Life a Little Easier'. Similarly, the stained glass windows designed by Timothy Newman for the Waikīkī Resort Hotel, the carved door at the Aloha Surf Hotel's Surf Lounge, the mural in the

The scene at Jack-in-the-Box located under the Hyatt Regency parking facility.

Mural at 1877 Kalākaua Avenue executed by Lillie Mae James on the wall of the Wave Waikīkī nightclub.

The Hawaiian Humpback Whales mural, painted by Wyland in 1985, sets the 'Ilikai Hotel's Marina Tower apart from the crowd.

Lillie Mae James' wave mural on the 'Ewa wall of the Wave Waikīkī.   **189**

Hamburger Mary's Organic Grill, at 2109 Kūhiō Avenue, is a lauhala lined, memorabilia bedecked bar and cafe, with an air of nostalgic decadence. It is what you always knew the original Trader Vic's was like.

Hyatt Regency Hotel's parking garage, or the etched-glass panel in The Winery at the Outrigger West Hotel, all transmit pulsations that inform people of their special Waikīkī situation. Equally effective interior decor such as the floral carpets at the Princess Ka'iulani Hotel or the lauhala-walled and memorabilia-bedecked Hamburger Mary's Organic Grill, further reinforce people's consciousness of their

The decor in Don the Beachcomber, a restaurant located in the Waikīkī Beachcomber Hotel, evokes the South Seas idyll.

Offering views of neither Diamond Head nor the beach, the Waikīkī Beach Apartments at 2569 Lemon Road is enhanced by images of both.

Hawai'i environment. Likewise, repeated encounters with innumerable rainbow-clad or Diamond Head-profiled signs and graphics serve the same purpose and also attest to the profound impact that the romantic mythos exerts on residents as well as visitors.

Mr. Magoo rides the waves on his pizza baked at 1980 Kalākaua Avenue.

192

The graphics adorning Maria's mobile hot dog truck evoke an image that belies its former life as a postal van.

A Newman window in the lobby of the Waikīkī Resort Hotel at Lili'uokalani and Koa Avenues.

A tropical leaf sign at the Pua-Lei-Lani Hotel at 250 Ka'iulani Avenue.

Inspired by Frank MacIntosh's 1930s Matson ocean liner menus, the sign for Ruffage Natural Foods at 2443 Kūhiō Avenue, is another by Lillie Mae James.

Couple these declarations of Hawai'i with the abundant vegetation, and over fifty waterways or fountains in Waikīkī, and the fact that neither Diamond Head nor the ocean are readily visible from the street becomes inconsequential. These strong images already are firmly engrained in the mind; they do not have to be seen to be believed. In their absence, the street plantings, weather, and architecture confirm their presence. Paradise lives in Waikīkī.

The Hippo hula girl sign at 468 'Ena Road. 193

A tropical paradise, a glamorous metropolis, and a carefree experience, present day Waikīkī scintillates with a multiplicity of alluring and somewhat contradictory images. Far greater than the sum of its parts, the district is the best of all worlds, a complex collage constructed out of the dreams and expectations of its visitors. Yet more than an image, Waikīkī is also an extremely attactive urban space. In striving to accommodate the idyllic intonations of the travel media, Waikīkī has developed many elements of an ideal cityscape. It is clean, green, and open, and extremely conducive to pleasant pedestrian experiences. It stands as a slightly overpopulated 'garden city'.

The beach as viewed from the Hawaiian Regent Hotel, a collage of complex images.

Part of the credit for this evolving environment must be given to the Waikīkī Special Design District Ordinance which the City and County of Honolulu passed in 1976. This law responded to demands by the tourist industry, through the Waikīkī Improvement Association, to institute quality control in Waikīkī. Mindful of the dangers of overdevelopment, the new ordinance cut the development potential of Waikīkī by 50%. It restricted hotel and apartment sizes and locations within the district, and emphasized the need for landscaped open space and a pedestrian-oriented environment. It required new developments to have at least 50% open space at the ground level, and established a minimum building setback from the street of 20 feet throughout the district, and 30 feet on Kalākaua Avenue, Kūhiō Avenue, Ala Wai Boulevard, Ala Moana Boulevard, and Kapahulu Avenue. It further required an additional one-foot setback for every ten feet that a building exceeded forty feet in height. The law also reduced the allowable capacities and heights of new buildings, and put in place sign regulations as well as architectural design review for all proposed projects.

The Royal Hawaiian Shopping Center, a series of low rise, garden courtyards and walkways placed on six and one half acres, was designed by architect Howard Wong. It well demonstrates the strong pedestrian orientation of Waikīkī. The black glass shop in the background houses Les Must de Cartier.

These regulations have promoted an open and varied streetscape, making Waikīkī a pedestrian paradise. The Kalākaua/Kūhiō activity hub, though highly developed, has an incredible amount of ground-level space directly accessible to people on foot. Doorless hotels and shopping complexes flow out and merge with the sidewalk. Expansive openings invite the casual stroller to depart from the sidewalk's 'straight and narrow', to wander and explore the spaces within and, not incidentally, examine the services and wares they have to offer.

Secluded stretchin' out at the Holiday Inn.

Life above the street at the Hyatt Regency.

In order to maintain such an extensive public space at ground level, Waikīkī hotels accommodate their more private activities at higher elevations. Frequently one discovers lobbies, swimming pools, intimate lounges and casual cafes catering to the hotel's clientele on upper floors. Because people are accustomed to the relegation of upper stories to more private uses, commercial ventures have encountered difficulties in attracting people to shops situated above the ground level. Entrepreneurs involved in Mitsukoshi, the Waikīkī Shopping Plaza, and the Royal Hawaiian Shopping Center have sadly learned that the higher you go, the less business you can anticipate. This retail difficulty is based not only on the recognition of upper stories as private activity areas, but also on the nature of consumerism in Waikīkī, and the fact that people comfortably situated in an attractive ground level setting are reticent to partake of vertical excursions.

The environment enhancing graphics beside the second floor pool at the Waikīkī Beachcomber Hotel were designed by Earl Honbo.

Looking down on the second floor pool at the Waikīkī Resort Hotel.

197

The lights, colors, exotic shops and carts, and plantings makes shopping in the International Market Place a show unto itself. This vibrant, outdoor shopping mecca, with such ancillary spin-offs as Duke's Lane, Waikīkī Flea Market, and Kūhiō Shopping Center adjoining it, never fails to entertain the casual stroller with its wide variety of goods, trinkets, jewelry, souvenirs, people and activities. A Waikīkī landmark, the International Market Place opened in 1957.

Shopping is a major recreational pastime in Waikīkī, as it is throughout America. However, in a paradise primarily populated by visitors, consumption is not a systematic or purposeful undertaking. Instead it is casual, informal, and impulsive. It is an immediate experience—a walk, see, stop, like, buy sequence of events. This 'we can just kinda amble' attitude has further encouraged a pedestrian oriented street-scape. Following the lead of the International Market Place, a network of quasi-alleys and passageways have developed throughout Waikīkī. Commercial niches, demarcated by a shift in paving materials, plantings, or spatial constrictions, offer wayfarers an intimacy not found on the street. They branch off the formal sidewalks and frequently parallel them, encouraging closer scrutiny of shops by the passerby.

Bargain basement stands and stores, and pornographic shops are scattered throughout Waikīkī in less advantageous locations.

To compete with such favorably situated shops, others either cater to more prurient interests or resort to fliers, hawkers, and/or large signs, that announce, frequently in red letters, sales and bargains. Littering the atmosphere, these efforts add to the total energy of Waikīkī, but are denounced as eyesores by those who evaluate them in terms of traditional aesthetics. Lacking any sense of subtlety, these blatant commercial gestures contribute little to the major mythic images of Waikīkī. However, they do toy with the vacationing imagination's love of a bargain and enjoyment of a freewheeling carnival atmosphere. Just as the midway with its Ferris wheel and sideshows served as an entertaining diversion for the multitudes who visited the 'Great White City' at the Chicago World's Exposition of 1893, so too these 'shoestring' operations have a place within the context of Waikīkī. Although from a theoretical point of view the area would be aesthetically better without them, Waikīkī's environment is too conducive to these enterprises to eliminate them. Furthermore, the methods used by these establishments keep everything in perspective. They prevent the surface of Waikīkī from becoming overly manicured or superficial in appearance. They are an everyday reality found in towns and cities across the nation, and they add another dimension to the pedestrian scene. An antidote to sterility, these commercial endeavors demand a different sort of involvement and human interaction.

201

Numerous open air cafes and restaurants, catering to a variety of tastes and pocketbooks, provide another level of interaction between pedestrian and environment.

The pedestrian orientation of the street contributes much to the retention of an intimate scale in Waikīkī, despite the presence of numerous high rises. This sense is further enhanced by a number of 'sidewalk cafes' or eating places that open onto the street, such as Popos Mexican Food, The Jolly Roger, and the Pizza Hut with its ill-proportioned iron fence, all of which line Kalākaua Avenue. Here, one step removed from the street, people sit, eat, and enjoy the bustle of others cruising by, realizing that they too have been a part of that crowd. In turn, the immediacy of people clustered about tables instills an unspoken interaction within the passersby that establishes a momentary rapport, a sharing that enhances the energies of all.

The Jolly Roger at 2244 Kalākaua Avenue.

The Burger King in the heart of Waikīkī at Lewers Street and Kalākaua Avenue, with the Royal Hawaiian Shopping Center across the street.

202

Busy Boy Cafe, at 371 'Olohana Street, with its rainbow of delights.

The lānai of the Monterey Bay Canners Seafood Restaurant and Oyster Bar on the second floor of the Outrigger Hotel provides a superb vista of the beach and the Royal Hawaiian Hotel.

he below street level Fuku-Chan restaurant a the Kotobuki Center at the corner of Koa nd Uluniu Avenues.

Similarly, peopled vantage points such as the Burger King at the corner of Lewers Street and Kalākaua Avenue, the Cock's Roost in the International Market Place, or the Monterey Bay Canners Fresh Seafood Restaurant overlooking the beach at the Outrigger Waikīkī Hotel, give the sensation of being above it all, but still very much a part of the scene. From below they remain distant, yet immediate, foci of activity. They invite people to look up and interact with their surroundings.

203

The Waikīkī Trade Center's 22-story tower viewed from the Waikīkī Market Place.

The thirty-six-story Diamond Head Vista apartments, at 2600 Pualani Way, is one of Waikīkī's more attractive high rises. Architect Warner Boone's placement of the lānai in a staggered pattern provides texture to this 1975 building's surface and tempers its vertical thrust.

The flat, slab high rise, when standing alone can add an element of drama to the skyline, as in this view of 2121 Ala Wai. However, when piled on top of each other such buildings lead to a blight of visual austerity.

Likewise, the high rise buildings themselves achieve a similar result, if they are visually stimulating. Canterbury Place with its soft, cream-colored, flowing lānai that gracefully articulate each story and its strong vertical elements perforated with 'portholes', (or are they 'tiny bubbles' percolating up from the Hilton Hawaiian Dome?) delights the eye with its play of light and shadow and diversity of form. Similarly, the striking silhouettes of the Waikīkī Trade Center, the Hyatt Regency towers, and Liliʻuokalani Gardens, and the smooth, pastel revelry of the Surfrider Hotel provide relief from the functional slab skyline. The sculptural character of these

Surfrider Hotel, designed by Wimberly, Whisenand, Allison, Tong & Goo in association with Roehrig, Onodera & Kinder, 1969.

Hilton Lagoon Apartments, designed by Bauer, Mori & Lum, 1967.

Leisure Heritage Apartments, designed by Wong & Wong, 1977.

Waikīkī Townhouse, designed by Jo Paul Rognstad, 1977.

Hawaiian Regent, designed by John Tatum and Chamberlain & Associates, 1971.

Princess Ka'iulani Hotel, designed by Gardner Dailey, 1955.

Perhaps the most optically enticing Waikīkī high rise, Canterbury Place at 1910 Ala Moana Boulevard was built in 1976 following the plans of architect Warner Boone.

buildings make distinct, statements that enhance the skyline, rather than merely intrude upon it. Other attempts to embellish the skyscape have included: the special handling of the lānai at the Princess Ka'iulani Hotel, Hilton Lagoon Apartments, and other structures; the late 1970s introduction of color to such buildings as the Royal Aloha Condominium, the Polynesian Aquacade, and Kūhiō Surf Club; and the occasional 1960s' use of restrained ornamentation as can be seen at the Kālia, the Waikīkī Skyliner, and at 2281 Ala Wai Boulevard. Such structures have attempted to foster within a high rise context some connection with the human condition. They,

A home in Deering Court greets the New Year.

Cleghorn Street apartments.

206

The district remains a place of contrasts in scale, use and images.

A vestige of the late nineteenth century, this house in Makaoe Lane is one of the few remaining in Honolulu with a separate cook house.

Another remnant of an earlier Waikīkī lifestyle, Manukai Street, stands juxtaposed to a highrise backdrop.

and many of their neighbors, have not always succeeded and, as a result, the presence of open space and small scale habitation areas continue to play a vital role in making Waikīkī a liveable and living area.

The Cooper Apartments and other garden/walkup apartments of the 1930s, as well as the remnants of Deering Court and other cottages, lie scattered throughout the backstreets of the district. They remain as vestiges of a less congested, and less security conscious Waikīkī. People obviously live and work within these structures,

Walkup apartments on Seaside Avenue.

A plantation style cottage on Hobron Lane.

Although smaller in area than Honolulu International Airport's reef runway, Waikīkī remains a city unto itself.

somehow eking out an existence in the shadow of the overwhelming towers which envelop their environment. Reassuringly, these low rise dwellings indicate to passersby that somehow life's normal routines do go on, albeit in some sort of detached fashion, even in Waikīkī. As reminders of the domestic, non-vacationing world, these structures serve as touchstones of reality: everyday people inhabit Waikīkī in an everyday way.

These buildings also invoke idyllic daydreams of a Waikīkī that perhaps, maybe, could have once existed: a small-scale, tropical paradise, where life slipped by in a carefree manner; a land of peace and plenty; a tranquil niche offering a verdant respite from the demands of the world. Similar flights of fancy are engendered by such small hotels as the Breakers, White Sands and Hawaiiana. These hostelries stand out as special places in which serenity of mind and scale are possible.

Combine the low rise oases of earlier times with the best of the more recent high rise developments, and Waikīkī extends a very positive environment to the visitor. The district meets its primary purpose—to fulfill the images engendered by advertising, television and word of mouth. More than any other area of intense development in Hawai'i, it keeps alive the sense of tropic wonder. Warm, bountiful, lively, and leisurely, it offers that rare opportunity to commune with nature in her most beneficent of moods, and to do so in the midst of an urban context. A city in its own right, Waikīkī pulsates with life on a superficial, but relaxing level. A land of high rises, it remains intimate, and, although an urban center, the usual tenseness, fear and loathing of the city are absent. It is a special design district in every sense of the word. Although enormously different from the remainder of Honolulu and Hawai'i, it offers much to the city, the state, and the world through its exotic variety and example.

Sunrise on Waikīkī Beach.

Tomorrow

A futuregraph of Kalākaua Ave.

Waikīkī Tomorrow
by Benjamin T. Torigoe

*D*oris Day once melodically reminded the American public that the future was not ours to see, so *que sera, sera*, whatever will be, will be. Despite such advice people repeatedly crystal ball gaze and plan for a better tomorrow, where their dreams will come true. A dream-come-true-land in its own right, Waikīkī seems to be very conducive to this sort of activity and a book on the famous beach cannot conclude without making some sort of gesture in the direction of answering the question, "What shall we do to improve Waikīkī?"

With at least a dozen plans already underwritten by the government to answer this question, one would think people would tire of asking; but such is not the case as indicated by the recent publication of the 'Waikīkī 2000' plan. To place this plan's objectives, and the Waikīkī of tomorrow, in a proper perspective, we should look at what planning has gone before. By considering what the past dreamed about today, we may achieve some enlightenment into our own visions of tomorrow.

Most of the current ideas relating to Waikīkī's future hark back to the thinking of earlier years and many were covered in the earliest published plan for Waikīkī, L.E. Pinkham's 1906 report to the Board of Health. One of the more feasible and far-sighted plans ever to be written on the district, this thirty-six page plan primarily sought to drain and fill the wetlands and fishponds of Waikīkī. The plan eventually achieved this goal, when the Ala Wai Canal was dredged between 1920 and 1928. However, with the exception of the canal's construction, the essence of the Pinkham Plan was not followed nor implemented, and to this day we are sadly reminded of this fact everytime it rains heavily in Waikīkī. Along with the non-construction of the drainage system envisioned by Pinkham, the following salient features also were never implemented:

1. The Ala Wai Canal was not completed back out to the sea on the Kapi'olani Park side, and the automatic tide gates that were to provide a natural flushing action were not constructed. As a result the canal stagnates and serves as a siltation basin which requires periodic dredging.

2. Boulevards and illumination along the canal were never completed for its entire length. Only the *mauka* shore, from the Ala Moana Bridge to Kalākaua Avenue were terraced and placed below grade, making a pleasant pedestrian area divorced from the street. Thus the potential of the canal as a park has been considerably diluted. Visions of a more parklike canal have recurringly reappeared, but so far to no avail. The Waikīkī 2000 Plan includes it as a hazy possible future improvement.

3. The enforcement of landscaped street setbacks of 45 and 25 feet for the main avenues and side streets, respectively. These were to be measured from the inner edge

A 'futuregraph' of Waikīkī rendered by A.S.
MacLeod in 1928 as the cover for the
Honolulu Advertiser's special edition on
Waikīkī. MacLeod's sketch essentially
embodied land speculators' enticing visions
of a more fully developed commercial strip
along Kalākaua Avenue resulting from the
completion of the Ala Wai Canal. Like
almost all conceptualizations of the future,
the picture merely transformed the current
scene into a more idealic state, in this
instance a downtown Honolulu streetscape
with a Diamond Head/Royal Hawaiian
backdrop.

The Royal Hawaiian and Moana hotels stand
as the only recognizable landmarks in an
otherwise transformed beach front in
Leonard Carey's depiction of Waikīkī, which
appeared in the 1947 Hawaiian Electric
publication, Honolulu of Tomorrow. A
more radical vision than that presented
twenty years earlier by MacLeod, this view
of tomorrow also incorporated the in-vogue
design trends of the time, but on a more
dramatic level. The City and County of
Honolulu has attempted to develop a
promenade along the ocean's edge, but their
attempt has been much less grandiose than
that envisioned by this illustration.

HAWAII
TOURISM...
...FUTURE
UNLIMITED

Pipe dream? Not at all.

Leading authorities on Hawaii tourism agree a scene like this is *quite likely* in the not-too-distant future.

Of all activity in Hawaii, tourism is the fastest growing and may hold the greatest promise for the future. Last year 171,588 visitors arrived here. By the time they left they had spent $82,700,000.

All predictions point to another record year in 1959. Estimates range from $95 to $100 million.

A Waikiki Beach that looks like this may please some people and disturb others. The plain economics of the matter is that Waikiki *is* going in this direction and the results, measured in new wealth circulated throughout the community, mean more prosperity, more employment, and a better standard of living for all Hawaii.

THE HAWAIIAN ELECTRIC CO., LTD. BUILDING TODAY FOR TOMORROW'S NEEDS

A view of Waikīkī imagined by the Hawaiian Electric company in their Paradise of the Pacific *advertisement of December 1960. This vision recognized the new high rise trend, but totally underestimated the extent to which this form would proliferate in the ensuing years.*

To the great surprise of the Honolulu community, Popular Mechanics *reported in 1912, "Businessmen of Honolulu, Hawaii are preparing to build a modern hotel on the reef off Diamond Head, where the naval station is located. The most interesting feature of the hotel will be a glass-walled shaft which will extend down into the sea, allowing the guests to descend and observe the wonderful sea life in that locality." This exploitation of the reef was not heard from again, but other schemes of that ilk have been suggested including, in recent years, a reef highway from the airport to Waikīkī.*

of the sidewalk, and were to be devoted solely to landscaping and trees. Sidewalks were to be of six foot width everywhere and eight feet wide along the canal. Since 1906, plans repeatedly have recommended setbacks in Waikīkī, but the Waikīkī Special Design District ordinance passed in 1974 has been the only attempt to implement these suggestions. Even this law is not as open-space minded as Pinkham's proposal; nor are the current 'Waikīkī 2000' visions.

4. Configuring the 'reclaimed' lands into 'superblocks' of 400 by 800 feet. This proposal has never been considered seriously, and more than likely never will be. Only rare private developments, such as Lili'uokalani Gardens, provide any evidence of the form Waikīkī might have assumed if this provision had been implemented at the time of the construction of the Canal.

5. Underground utilities for the entire district, easily accessible under the sidewalks. The implementation of this proposal has been partially accomplished through the piecemeal placement of lines beneath the streets, where maintenance and repair measures remain disruptive to traffic.

6. Promotion and encouragement of public motor vehicle/bus transportation over the use of private vehicles. A number of reports on the traffic problems in Waikīkī, including one in 1959 dealing strictly with this issue, have recommended similar measures, but none have yet been implemented. The Waikīkī 2000 Plan resurrects these previous visions in the form of a jitney service for the district.

A second and even greater visionary than Pinkham, Lewis Mumford, the internationally noted authority on city and regional planning, came to Honolulu at the invitation of the City and County of Honolulu Park Board. In 1938 Mumford produced for the Board a sixty-seven page report, *A Memorandum Report on Park and City Planning—Whither Honolulu?*, which covered "general planning for the city and county of Honolulu in addition to parks". The plan touched on a number of recommendations applicable to Waikīkī, and stressed the fact that:

> *Whatever is done toward urban improvements should be done well. It should be done not by mere rote and habit, as cheaply as possible, as conventionally as possible. It should be done rather out of the fullest inquiry into the best contemporary city planning methods, and out of the fullest determination to achieve the sort of political organization that is necessary to put such a project through.*

A major recommendation of Mumford's plan required a study of the natural City zones—port zone, industrial zone, central shopping zone, administrative zone, recreation zone and residential zone. He found that, "the chain of parks that now begins with Ala Moana and passes along the shore area through Kapi'olani Park and the intermittent connecting patches along Waikīkī . . . , together with the Ala Wai and the yacht basin at the end, transform the immediate neighborhood into what one may properly call the recreation zone of Honolulu." A plan to develop this area for recreation use, although called for in Mumford's proposal, has never been articulated. The Waikīkī Special Design District considers a portion of this area, but in terms beyond, and almost irrelevant to, recreational values. The Waikīkī 2000 Plan addresses recreation concerns only for Kapi'olani Park, and does this against Mumford's advice to avoid makeshift park developments.

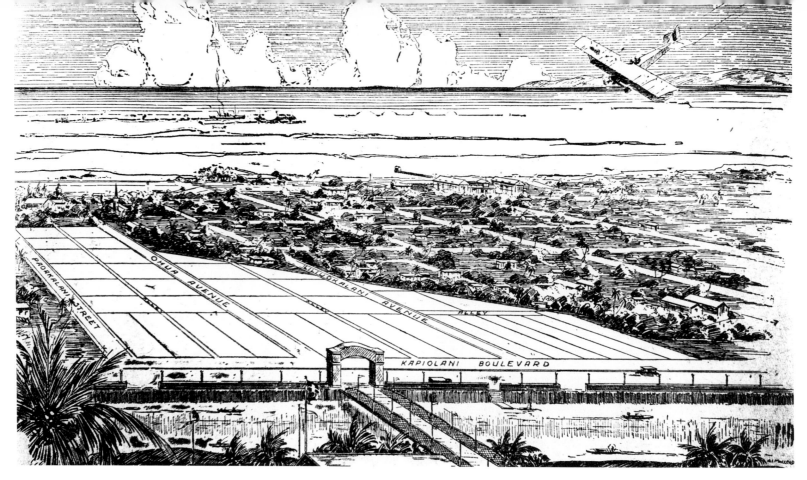

In the illustration labels: PAOAKALANI STREET, OHUA AVENUE, TUSITALA, LILIUOKALANI AVENUE, ALLEY, KAPIOLANI BOULEVARD

The idea of another bridge spanning the Ala Wai Canal has been a recurring one. This 1924 flight of fancy by A.S. MacLeod to promote the opening of the McCarthy subdivision might be the initial impetus for the idea. Hopefully, it is an idea whose time will never come.

In essence, Pinkham and Mumford's plans called for the preservation of a parklike open, tropical atmosphere in Waikīkī; the servicing of the district by adequate and properly maintained public infrastructures; and convenient access. Much of what they envisioned has only been minutely implemented, and then, when done, undertaken without the clarity, commitment to action and quality that Mumford declared would be required.

Throughout the 1950s–1970s plans for Waikīkī have recurringly formulated scenarios similar to those of Pinkham and Mumford, although usually in much more expansive and expensive reports. Commencing with a 1954 traffic and planning study prepared for the County Planning Commission, the State and City governments actively concerned themselves with the quality, character and density of development in Waikīkī. From 1954 onward a veritable stream of plans continually warned of the adverse effects of uncontrolled growth in the district in relationship to its streets, roads, sewers and building densities and heights, and the wanton extent to which the area was being permitted to be developed.

In 1964, the Planning Department hired a consultant to prepare 'The Waikīkī Plan', which proposed to control growth and development in the Waikīkī-Diamond Head

The Kamehameha Investment Company, anticipating the development of Bishop Estate's lands fronting on Kalākaua Avenue, co-sponsored with the Hawai'i Chapter of the American Institute of Architects an ideas competition in 1973. They received a number of entries, some of which were quite bold, and appeared to follow Lewis Mumford's suggestion to express the best ideals of Hawai'i through the transformation of Waikīkī's environment.

None of the proposals submitted for the competition were implemented and the Royal Hawaiian Shopping was built. The following submittals reveal alternate thoughts on a Waikīkī that could have been, and may yet be.

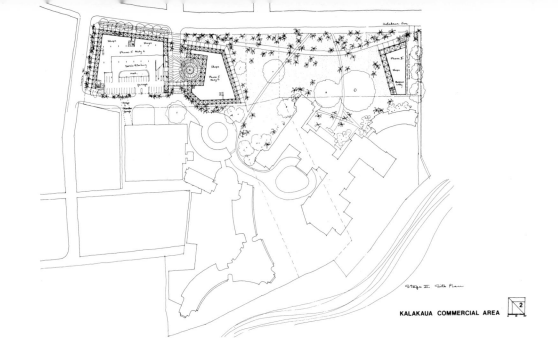

KALAKAUA COMMERCIAL AREA

The firm of Charles Sutton and Associates won the competition on the strength of these designs. The proposal allowed for a large green open space, shopping, offices and parking on the premises.

Lewis Mumford: A Different Tomorrow

*L*ewis Mumford arrived in Honolulu on 15 June 1938, to be the principal speaker at the Pacific Conference of the New Education Fellowship at the University of Hawai'i. He came to the Islands as a nationally renowned author and lecturer, with a reputation based on his numerous articles in such magazines as *Dial, The American Mercury, Harper's* and *Scribner's,* and his seven books, including his most recent *Culture of Cities.*

The forty-two year old social analyst, philosopher, and critic of art and architecture remained in Honolulu for ten days, and besides giving two lectures at the New Education Fellowship Conference, was interviewed by KGU and addressed a Hawai'i Housing Authority luncheon at the Alexander Young Hotel. In the course of his stay he praised the Honolulu Academy of Arts for its human scale, simplicity of line, oriental influences, and adaptation to Hawai'i's climate. To the Hawai'i Housing Authority, which was in the midst of deciding how to approach the design of low-cost public housing, he recommended that they consider erecting buildings suitable to Hawai'i's climate and the Island style of life. For Mumford this meant single-story, single-family, frame dwellings built on concrete piers, with wide, overhanging rooflines and many windows.

As a result of Mumford's talks, Lester McCoy, the head of the City and County's Parks Department, invited the noted author to return to Honolulu to undertake a study of Honolulu's parks. After some consideration, Mumford agreed and returned to Hawai'i with his wife and two children at the beginning of August 1938, to vacation and undertake the study.

During his second stay in the Islands Mumford commented on a number of issues facing Honolulu beyond that of its recreation concerns. He found Waikīkī already too intensely developed, and predicted that the district soon would become a "Hawaiian type of Coney Island". He voiced opposition to "unnecessary and expensive hillside subdivisions", and the construction of the Pali tunnel as both endeavors only promoted the "aimless spreading out of the population." He spoke in favor of open space, tree lined streets, the construction of Ala Moana Boulevard, the construction of additional canals such as the Ala Wai and Kapalama, and the expansion of Waikīkī Beach from Ala Moana Park to Koko Head.

On 9 September 1938, Mumford and his family departed Hawai'i on the *Lurline.* Three months later his report, 'Whither Honolulu?' was released. The *Star-Bulletin* indicated the report elicited different points of view from the citizenry of Hawai'i. Some felt the report disclosed that, "Honolulu is going to the demnition bowwows;" others found the report "largely impractical;" while still another segment of the population hailed Mumford as a "major prophet". The newspaper, itself, found the report to be "stimulating reading", but suggested that critical readers might "find

Lewis Mumford made the cover of Time *magazine just prior to coming to Hawai'i.*

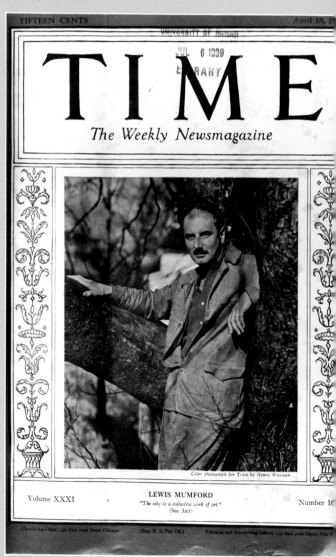

Mumford admired the parklike setting along the Ala Wai canal and recommended that it be completed for the length of the canal, and emulated in other sections of Honolulu.

much of it as far short of the practical as a Maxfield Parrish dream picture is short of stern reality. But he [Mumford] paints a picture of 'what can be' with all the brilliant and intriguing colors of a Maxfield Parrish print."

The most outspoken critic of 'Whither Honolulu?' was Louis Cain, the City and County's Superviser of Public Works, who labeled the report "sixty-seven pages of Mr. Mumford's mumblings". He found the report to be based on inaccurate information, its premises to be vague and unsound, and its recommendations to be impracticable and impossible. Among other items, Cain questioned Mumford's assumption that Honolulu's population of approximately 180,000 was about to stabilize (Cain saw it as possibly doubling), and also criticized Mumford's recommendation for water controls and his anti-billboard position. In conclusion the public works administrator felt, "Mr. Mumford has some good suggestions but the whole report must be very carefully analyzed before attempting what he suggests. My own opinion is we could profitably forget it."

The report unfortunately did go unheeded, and in 1947 the *Honolulu Advertiser* declared the dollars spent on the report to have been wasted as "no attention was paid to that very thoughtful, penetrating analysis which now languishes on the shelves of persons who were fortunate enough to latch onto one."

Mumford, himself, fared much better than 'Whither Honolulu?'. Following the report he went on to write approximately two dozen more books, and to hold professorships at Stanford, the University of Pennsylvania and the University of California at Berkeley, despite the fact that he never graduated from college. He has received innumerable honors and awards, and is recognized as one of the preeminent spokesmen of the twentieth century.

219

Group Seventy architects went beyond considering the Bishop Estate parcel, and proposed the non-development of the land as a first step in transforming Waikīkī's beachfront into a lush open space.

1900

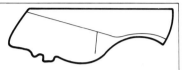

In 1900, the only land given to the automobile was a dirt road known as 'Waikīkī Road' and a small side street called 'Lewers Road'. Around this began the growth, unprecendented in the history of Waikīkī.

1925

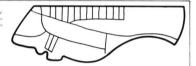

By 1925, the car began to demand land, and with the dredging of the Ala Wai Canal, some of the major streets began to crisscross Waikīkī . . . the pattern of future crisis was emerging.

1950 saw the basic pattern of streets well established and the construction of a few parking garages—foretelling what was to come in the next two decades . . . the complete takeover of the vehicle and its demands.

1970

Today, the car has all but choked off any resemblance to what Waikīkī was, or should be, covering the land like a black blight, producing noise, air pollution, heat, traffic snarls, short tempers, etc., and eliminating the open spaces that are so precious!

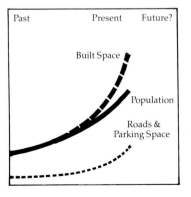

220

area. The 1969 Waikīkī Task Force continued the planning process by again investigating the area, and prepared a report through the Hawai'i Visitors Bureau's Statewide Goals Committee. Like previous studies this one concluded that Waikīkī was overzoned and the area's infrastructure and public support facilities were totally inadequate and had not kept up with the rampant growth in the district. Similar concerns and opinions were reiterated in the 1970 Planning Department's study to City Council, the 1971 report from the Mayor's Planning Advisory Committee for the Waikīkī-Diamond Head area, and the November 1973 Temporary Visitor Industry Council report.

All these plans for the future finally led to the adoption of the Waikīkī Special Design District Ordinance on 1 April 1974. No April Fools' Day joke, even though it represented the culmination of at least twenty years of *only* studying the area, this ordinance, took a large step forward, and incorporated, to varying degrees, select ideas intially presented by Pinkham, Mumford, and the 1954 report.

Even after the passage of the Special Design District ordinance, plans continued to flow in an apparent knee-jerk manner. Both Professor Robert Freilich's 25 July 1974 report to the City Council establishing "a sound future for Waikīkī through density and planning controls", and the Department of General Planning's $300,000 study, *Volume I, Summary and Issues and Methodology for Urban Design and Economic Modeling in the Waikīkī Area,* submitted on 11 April 1975, were essentially after-the-fact plans, as their major features had already been implemented in the Waikīkī Special Design District ordinance.

From the experience of the past it becomes obvious that recommendations for a better tomorrow come easily, but their implementation is a difficult, if not impossible task. Because of the pressures of economics, vested interests, politics, and whatever, the what 'could be' for Waikīkī has been ignored and rejected. The seemingly eternal interplay between what people should do and what they want to do, forever remains the tricky gap to be negotiated along the path from dream to actuality.

The most recent plan for Waikīkī, 'Waikīkī 2000', an implementation program and plan of action that would "reorient Waikīkī back to the people and to make it a more pedestrian-oriented place", attempts to bridge this gap. As with previous plans it calls for: 1. discouraging further expansion of apartments, hotels and commercial areas in Waikīkī; 2. upgrading of sidewalks, roadways, street lighting/graphics/furniture system, sewers and storm drains; 3. improving and upgrading the vehicular circulation system by widening Kūhiō Avenue, making a partial pedestrian mall for Kalākaua Avenue, and providing new and/or improved parking and park-and-ride facilities; 4. establishing a major beautification program through landscaping; and 5. establishing pedestrian walkways, esplande and bikeways along the shoreline and in Waikīkī, including a new pedestrian bikeway bridge over the Ala Wai Canal from Mō'ili'ili.

As an action plan, Waikīkī 2000 has merit. By specifically calling for the implementation of programs to fulfill long needed improvements, it has, in certain areas, worked effectively. It has the power of execution that so many plans of the past have not had. However, a lot of room exists for non-fulfillment, and even more room for feeble implementation, and gesture-like action which in the long term will require redoing. Some aspects of the Waikīkī 2000 plan need re-examination, as they either have not been done well and/or lack the "innovation to conceive and the courage to desire". These include:

1. During the design of the Kūhiō Avenue widening and especially after its completion, the inadequate sidewalk area and width were borne out. For a street of such magnitude and major use by pedestrians, the miniscule width of 4 feet clear from any appurtenants such as fire hydrants, street trees, street signs and light poles, is totally inappropriate. Also, the street beautification program along Kūhiō, in comparison to that along Punahou Street and Kapi'olani Boulevard, leaves the impression of makeshift, afterthought improvements.

2. The Gateway Park project, if completed, is not inviting; it does not say 'Welcome to Waikīkī and Aloha'. An open space with trees, flowers, walkway or paths, and a sign does not constitute by itself a 'Gateway Park'. Half of the problem of doing something, is doing it well.

3. The Queen Kapi'olani Park Master Plan, completed in 1983 as a component in the implementation of Waikīkī 2000, also stirs concerns with regard to how well the plan will be implemented. This plan contains no provision for the formulation and adoption of a detailed maintenance organization and management plan for its implementation.

4. The proposed pedestrian/bikeway bridge across the Ala Wai Canal from Mō'ili'ili is an idea that has been hashed over and over again. Each time to the judgment of good city planning, common sense and a sensitivity and appreciation of beauty and aesthetics, the idea has been overwhelmingly rejected. This is an idea whose time should never come. On its face and on its merits, it is a BAD idea. One need only stand on the bridge over the Ala Wai at McCully Street, and see the sunrise and sunset to clearly understand why it is a poor idea and why Lewis Mumford uttered, "Waikīkī short-cut not needed."

Waikīkī 2000 holds the potential to render dramatic changes to Waikīkī. In trying to implement this plan's proposals or, for that matter, any thoughts on tomorrow's Waikīkī, we might best recall Lewis Mumford's admirable 1938 summary of Honolulu, which is appropriate to Waikīkī as well:

No other city that I know would proportionately yield such high returns to rational planning as Honolulu. But the necessary impulse, the necessary popular support, will be lacking so long as Honolulu's citizens seek merely to maintain the system of familiar compromises, evasions, and negligences that are recorded in the present state of Honolulu. And in the end, who loves his city best?—he who seeks to improve it, or he who is content to muddle along in the familiar grooves, exercising a minimum of foresight, intelligence, and imagination? HISTORY ALLOWS NO DOUBT AS TO THE ANSWER: THAT WHICH MAKES A CITY DEAR TO LATER GENERATIONS IS THE POWER TO MASTER ITS OWN DESTINY AND EXPRESS ITS BEST IDEALS IN THE TRANSFORMATION OF ITS ENVIRONMENT.

VERBUMSAP

1972

Regeneration of Beneficial Public Open Space

Landholders will be selected to participate in a trend-reversing history-making environmental experiment. Through selected purchase and building demolition, currently misused beach lands will be transformed by a State Trust to the highest beneficial use for the public, all windfalls, accruing to the Trust.

A moratorium on new building pending new Master Plan.

PHASE I
THE BISHOP ESTATE
BEGINNING, A 20TH
CENTURY
KAMEHAMEHA MAHELE

1980

Expansion

Ongoing review of zoning ordinances, land coast, etc. in Waikiki and Islands-wide to assure beneficial use of the land.

Tourism and Land Development will come under careful management, private profit notwithstanding, to guarantee livelihood without abuse of the land.

PHASE II
1980 MAJOR FEDERAL
LAND GRANT

1990

A Master Plan for Tourism

A Master Plan for Tourism having been developed, establishment of stabilization policy for resident and tourist population.

A Master Plan for transoceanic, inter-island and intra-island transportation. Outer Island airports for transoceanic flights.

Built areas reviewed and density controlled. Open space developed as informal parks and auto parking.

PHASE III
CONTINUAL ACQUISITION OF VESTPOCKET
PARCELS

2000

Islands-wide General Acceptance of Opened Space Goal

Accelerated acquisition of Private Parcels. Probable private land gifts and grants to the State Trust.

Watchdog control in perpetuity of Open Space Preservation regardless of future technological change.

PHASE IV
WAIKIKI DEMONSTRATION 'CLIMAX'
OPEN SPACE

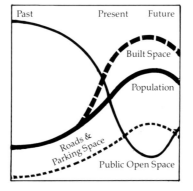

Reference Notes

The Seat of Power

3 "while away the time.": John Papa Ī'ī, "Fragments of Hawaiian History", (Bernice Pauahi Bishop Museum, Honolulu, 1959) pp. 92-93

"The event of each morning . . . ": Harriet Newell Foster Deming, "Years of Sunshine Days, Memories of a Childhood in Hawaii", Hawaiian Mission Children's Society, unpublished manuscript, no date, p. 94

"The natives in the . . . " *ibid*, p. 128

5 seven heiau in Waikīkī: Thomas G. Thrum, "Tales from the Temples", in *The Hawaiian Annual 1907*, pp. 44-45

"During the plague . . . ": Thomas G. Thrum, "Leahi Heiau: Papaenaena", in *The Hawaiian Annual 1926*, pp. 111-112

More information on the Wizard Stones can be found in James H. Boyd, "The Tradition of Ka-Pae-Mahu", *The Hawaiian Annual 1907*, pp. 139-141

7 "Aloha Kou e . . . ": Abraham Fornander, *Hawaiian Antiquities and Folklore* vol. V, no. 1, Honolulu, 1918-1919, pp. 30-31

Victorian Waikīkī — The Playground of Royalty

8 Hamohamo's transfer to Lili'uokalani is recorded in Book 12, page 26 in the Bureau of Conveyances.

9 "falling into rapid decay" and "vestige of ancient times": G.W. Gates, *Sandwich Island Notes* (New York: Harper Brothers, 1854), pp. 93-94; "historic Waikīkī": A. Grove Day: *Mark Twain's Letters from Hawaii* (New York: Appleton-Century, 1966), p. 52

10 Bishop residence, making "it into a large . . .": Harold Winfield Kent, *Charles Reed Bishop—Man of Hawaii* (Palo Alto, California: Pacific Books, 1965), p. 36

Kamehameha V's acquisition of Helumoa is recorded in Book 20, page 204, and Book 40, page 221 in the Bureau of Conveyances.

11 Kalākaua's purchase of Uluniu is recorded in Book 64, page 127 in the Bureau of Conveyances.

11 "white frame structure . . . ": Mary H. Krout, *Hawaii and the Revolution, the Personal Experiences of a Correspondent in the Sandwich Islands During the Crisis of 1893 and Subsequently* (New York: Dodd and Mead, 1898), p. 104

"Aboard the boat . . . ": William T. Brigham, "Charles Reed Bishop 1822-1915", *Hawaiian Annual for 1916*, p. 67, 68

12 For additional biographical information on A. S. Cleghorn see: *Pacific Commercial Advertiser*, June 18, 1901, p. 5; and Dorothea Woodrum, *Governor Cleghorn, Princess Kaiulani and Ainahau* (Honolulu: Island Development Corporation, 1964)

Woodrum, on pp. 6-7 of *Governor Cleghorn* . . . incorrectly claimed that Princess Ruth Ke'elikolani presented Cleghorn's daughter, Princess Ka'iulani, with 'Āinahau as a christening gift on Christmas day 1875. Princess Ruth gave Ka'iulani only 3.91 acres of land that provided 'Āinahau with access to Waikīkī Road via the street now known as Ka'iulani Avenue. See Book 34, page 392 in the Bureau of Conveyances for the original transfer of 'Āinahau to Cleghorn by Ma'aua and Koihala, and Book 44, page 219 for the conveyance of Princess Ruth's gift.

"the most beautiful . . .": *Paradise of the Pacific*, March 1904, p. 10. For another description of the estate see the *Pacific Commercial Advertiser*, June 9, 1877, and also Else Waldron, *Honolulu 100 Years Ago* (Honolulu, 1967), pp. 101-106.

13 "strangely agitated" and "A gentleman of": *Pacific Commercial Advertiser*, November 6, 1910, p. 1

"came as a severe shock . . . ": *Pacific Coast Advertiser*, January 25, 1917. The opening of the subdivision was reported in the *Pacific Coast Advertiser*, May 1, 1919.

14 "too glary": Una Hunt Drage, *Hawaii Deluxe*, a compilation of her diaries and letters, 1901, unpublished manuscript, Mission Houses Museum Library, p. 86

"the quiet life of Waikīkī . . . ": Harriet Newell Foster Deming, "Years of Sunshine Days, Memories of a Childhood in Hawaii", Hawaiian Mission Children's Society, unpublished manuscript, no date, p. 112

"Went out to Waikīkī . . . ": and following quotations from Queen Lili'uokalani's Diary, 1885, February 7, 11, 20, and April 2. Microfilm, Bishop Museum Library

14 "Displaying Hawaiian athletic . . .": Bernice Pi'ilani Irwin, *I Knew Queen Liliuokalani* (Honolulu: South Sea Sales, 1960), p. 26

"Why did the girls . . .": *ibid*, p. 82

"The Boat House . . .": Nelly Strickland, "Notes of a Journey", *Chicago Evening Post*, May 5, 1890

"everything that can be . . .": Una Hunt Drage, *Hawaii Deluxe*, a compilation of her diaries and letters, 1901, unpublished manuscript, Mission Houses Museum Library, p. 70

16 The lū'au for the Duke of Edinburgh was reported in the *Hawaiian Gazette*, July 28, 1869 and the *Pacific Commercial Advertiser*, July 31, 1869.

17 "people of wealth . . .": Burton Holmes, "Social Life in Honolulu", *Paradise of the Pacific*, February 1899, p. 17

"Quaint Japanese maids . . .": *ibid*, p. 18

"Suck one's fingers . . .": *ibid*, p. 18

"blazing torch . . ." Maude Jones, "Kaiulani—Personal Glimpses of a Princess," File #6 (147), Daughters of Hawai'i, unpublished manuscript. White muslin dust catchers were ruffles sewn to the bottom of gowns to protect their lovely silk or moiré material.

"hoydenish, cracking away . . .": Una Hunt Drage, *Hawaii Deluxe*, a compilation of her diaries and letters, 1901, unpublished manuscript, Mission Houses Museum Library, p. 70

"half-hearted dips": Mrs. G.P. Andrews, "Life at Waikiki", *Paradise of the Pacific*, March 1896, p. 34

"The week of the full moon . . .": Drage, *op. cit.*, p. 37

19 "About ten days ago . . . ": letter from Princess Ka'iulani to Queen Lili'uokalani, January 5, 1899, Hawaii State Archives

From Mosquitoes to Mansions

21 "becoming a considerable place of resort . . . ": *Biennial Report of the Minister of the Interior to the Legislature of 1860*, p. 19. For a description of the new foreign community see Deming, "Years of Sunshine Days".

22 "quite a little community . . . ": *Pacific Commercial Advertiser* September 16, 1865, p.2 c.1

22 "a hamlet of plain cottages . . . ": William R. Bliss, *Paradise in the Pacific* (New York: Sheldon & Company, 1873), pp. 195-196

A discussion of the difficulty to procure water appears in Deming, "Years of Sunshine Days", pp. 93, 128.

23 For more information on the introduction of mosquitoes in 1826 see D. Elmo Hardy, *Insects of Hawaii*, vol. 10 (Honolulu: University of Hawai'i Press, 1960) p. 18.

"There are a good many mosquitoes . . . ": A. Grove Day: *Mark Twain's Letters from Hawaii* (New York: Appleton-Century, 1966), p.3

"seaside felicity . . . ": George Leonard Chaney, *Aloha! A Hawaiian Salutation* (Boston: Roberts Brothers, 1879), p. 25

"during whose reign . . . ": Senate Joint Resolution #5 of March 14, 1905

24 For more information on the counterrevolution see Albertine Loomis, *For Whom Are the Stars?* (Honolulu: University Press of Hawai'i, 1976).

27 The Hustace residence's history and demolition was reported in the *Honolulu Advertiser*, October 3, 1950, p. 10. Other information obtained from conveyance documents.

28 "transforming this section of town . . .": *The Hawaiian Annual for 1901*, p.172

"an ideal Waikīkī residence . . . ": *Pacific Commercial Advertiser*, October 4, 1899, p.1

31 The Steiner residence history and demolition appeared in the *Honolulu Advertiser*, April 2, 1960, p. A-15. Other information obtained from original blueprints.

36 The *Star Bulletin*, July 30, 1961, mag. section, p. 30 discussed the 1944 stay of Franklin D. Roosevelt at Queen Surf. Other information on the house may be found in *Honolulu Advertiser* March 26, 1961, mag. section, p. 32.

37 The transfer of Kealohilani to Kūhiō is recorded in Book 488, page 299 in the Bureau of Conveyances. The June 25, 1918 *Pacific Commercial Advertiser* reported the settlement, and noted that the Trust also agreed to either sell Washington Place to the Territory or make it into a Lili'uokalani Memorial.

38 "Moloch of modernism . . .": *Paradise of the Pacific*, February 1922. The sale of the house was covered for one month in both the *Honolulu Advertiser* and *Star Bulletin*, commencing March 16, 1935. The demolition of Kūhiō's home was noted in *The Hawaiian Annual for 1937*, p. 79.

40 "foremost financier . . . ": *Honolulu Star-Bulletin*, October 22, 1963, p. 1

Kapi'olani Park

42 "From an early hour . . . " *Pacific Commercial Advertiser*, June 16, 1877, p. 3 c. 6

"A tract of land in the vicinity . . . " Charter, Kapi'olani Park Association Incorporation, December 1, 1876 can be found in the Interior Department Book 14, p. 205, Hawai'i State Archives. For a history of the Park see *Pacific Commercial Advertiser*, November 11, 1876, p.2 c.3, and *The Hawaiian Annual for 1910*, pp. 139-141.

43 One perspective on the history of Camp McKinley is capsulized in L. A. Thurston's letter of October 21, 1898 to General Charles King and in subsequent correspondence, *Kapiolani Park Association Minutes and Correspondence*, vol. 1 no. 1, pp. 236-242, Hawai'i State Archives.

46 The opening of the aquarium and its history was covered in the *Pacific Commercial Advertiser*, March 20, 1904, p. 5.

48 Information on the start of the zoo may be found in E.J. Botts, "A Jolly, Necessary Zoo", *Paradise of the Pacific*, December 1917, pp. 48-49; *Pacific Commercial Advertiser*, December 28, 1916, p. 2; and *The Annual Report of the Parks Committee, City & County of Honolulu for 1916* (Honolulu: 1917). For Daisy's arrival and demise see *Pacific Commercial Advertiser* for August 19, 1916, p. 7; September 7, 1916, p. 9; September 11, 1916, p. 7; February 22, 1933, editorial; February 23, 1933, editorial; February 28, 1933, p. 1; March 4, 1933, p. 1.

50 Information on the War Memorial Natatorium can be found in Ralph S. Kuykendall and Lorin Tarr Gill, *Hawaii in the World War*, Honolulu, 1928, pp. 447-454, and in the *Honolulu Advertiser* August 24, 1927 through August 29, 1927.

51 Information on the dedication and demolition of the Phoenix Fountain can be found in *Honolulu Advertiser* March 17, 1919, p.1 and *Honolulu Star-Bulletin* and *Honolulu Advertiser* from November 10, 1942 through December 15, 1942.

Bathhouses and Hostelries

52 References to Brighton, Newport and Trouville can be found in *Paradise of the Pacific*, January 1888, p.4, and Henry Martyn Whitney, *The Tourists' Guide Through the Hawaiian Islands* (Honolulu: 1890), p.12.

"With the exception of . . .": Charles Nottage, *In Search of a Climate* (London: S. Low, Marston & Co., 1894) p.44

"Here the tourist may lave . . .": *Paradise of the Pacific*, May 1892, p.4

53 Information relating to the Long Branch Baths and its toboggan may be found in *Pacific Commercial Advertiser*, December 24, 1881, p. 3 c. 6; January 14, 1882 p.5; January 28, 1882, p.3 c.6; and May 22, 1889, p. 2 c. 3; and *Daily Bulletin* May 17, 1889, p. 3 c. 3.

The Waikīkī Beach Company's deed for the Waikīkī Inn is recorded at the Bureau of Conveyances in Book 193, page 432.

54 The declaration that the Waikīkī Villa was "Very commodious," was made in *Paradise of the Pacific*, January 1888.

55 No hotel at Waikīkī: *Hawaiian Gazette*, August 3, 1881

"As yet there is no hotel . . .": *Paradise of the Pacific*, January 1888, p.4

Taking into account that, historically, Waikīkī encompassed a far greater area than it does today, one might claim the first Waikīkī hotel to be the Hotel at Waikīkī operated by John Mitchener. The hotel consisted of a complex of adobe structures including a "dwelling house, store and cook house" [*Polynesian*, March 6, 1847, p. 171 c. 3], and was located near the present intersection of King Street and Kalākaua Avenue, on the approximate location of the First Hawaiian Bank. The proprietor was an Englishman who had come to Hawai'i in the mid-1820s and had married Kaioe. Richard Brinsley Hind, a surgeon on the ship *Sulpher*, described Mitchener in July 1837 as "a respectable man, . . . now compelled to keep a billiard table through misfortunes." The hotel advertised a bowling alley and "such other facilities for amusement and recreation as will tend to add to the comfort of gentlemen." The advertisement claimed horses and carriages would be "carefully attended", the table supplied "with the choicest viands", and the bar "constantly furnished with the best wines and liquors". Furthermore the public was advised, "a short notice will ensure the most extensive arrangements for the gratification of visitors" [*Sandwich Island Gazette*, July 22, 1837 p. 1, c. 3] Opening in 1837, this venture was short-lived, as in April 1838 Mitchener's advertisement disappeared from the newspaper, and in 1842 the property was put up for sale. Mitchener died in Honolulu on June 20, 1862 [*Polynesian*, June 21, 1862].

55 Information on the Park Beach Hotel can be found in *Paradise of the Pacific*, July 1888, p.4, and May 1889, p.5, and *The Hawaiian Directory and Handbook of the Kingdom of Hawaii* (San Francisco: McKenney Directory Company, 1888), p. 54.

57 For a history of the Sans Souci Hotel see Dorothea Woodrum, *Historic Sans Souci* (Honolulu, 1960). For other information on the hotel see *Pacific Commercial Advertiser*, June 6, 1884; and *Paradise of the Pacific*, February 1894 where p. 21 makes the "beau ideal . . ." statement. For information on Robert Louis Stevenson at the Sans Souci see Sister Martha Mary McGaw, *Stevenson in Hawaii* (Honolulu: University of Hawai'i Press, 1950), pp. 115-117.

"If anyone desires . . ." Sister Martha Mary McGaw erroneously reports in *Stevenson in Hawaii* that the Sans Souci used this ledger inscription in its advertisements in Honolulu's daily newspapers for three days. However, the advertisement appeared only in the *Daily Bulletin* and ran from October 30, 1893 until August 10, 1894, when the Sans Souci discontinued advertising in this newspaper.

58 "truly Bohemian, with no pretense . . .": *Scribner's*, vol. LXXX, August 1926, p. 140

59 "the costliest and . . .": *The Hawaiian Annual for 1901*, pp. 161-165

For descriptions of the Moana Hotel see *Pacific Commercial Advertiser*, March 12, 1901, p. 2, and *The Hawaiian Annual for 1901*, pp. 161-165.

61 The construction of the Moana's wings was covered in *Pacific Commercial Advertiser*, February 28, 1918, p. 6. For information on the pier see *Paradise of the Pacific*, October 1930, p. 3, and *Honolulu Advertiser*, August 28, 1930, p. 1 c. 3.

62 "the finest part . . .": *Husted's Directory of Honolulu and the Territory of Hawaii: 1907* (Honolulu: Mrs. F. M. Husted, 1907), p. 11

63 Information on the opening of the Honolulu Seaside Hotel can be located in *The Hawaiian Annual for 1907*, p. 153; *Pacific Commercial Advertiser*, April 11, 1906, p. 9 c. 2, April 15, 1906, p. 2 c. 3-4, and May 6, 1906, p. 5 c. 5.

64 The closing of the Seaside Hotel was discussed in *The Hawaiian Annual for 1925*, p. 122 and *Honolulu Advertiser*, July 29, 1925, p. 10 c. 3.

Information on Alice Roosevelt's stays in Hawai'i may be found in *Pacific Commercial Advertiser* and *Star Bulletin* of July 14-15, 1905, and *Paradise of the Pacific* July 1905, p. 16 and September 1907, p. 9.

66 "one of the shrewdest . . .": *Pacific Coast Commercial Record*, May 1892, p. 17

68 For information on the Waikīkī Inn see *The Hawaiian Annual for 1914*, p. 66, and *Honolulu Advertiser*, July 25, 1918, p. 6 c. 2 and November 11, 1928, the Society Section, p. 15. The privileges cancelled by the liquor license commission had allowed the Waikīkī Inn to serve liquor with meals on Sundays during the hours 6:30-8:00 AM, 11:30 AM-2:00 PM, and 5:30-9:00 PM, and on other days until 1:00 AM instead of the regular closing time of 11:30 PM. Besides the Waikīkī Inn, the Moana and Young Hotels also had these privileges. For more information see *Star-Bulletin* June 27, 1913, p. 2 c. 5.

The Pierpoint Hotel's sale to J.F. Child was noted in *The Hawaiian Annual for 1923*, p. 144.

71 The Promotion Committee Report on Hotel Rooms, published in *Pacific Commercial Advertiser*, January 13, 1913, p. 7, disclosed the following Waikīkī room counts—hotels: Moana, 150; Seaside, 60; boarding houses: Waikīkī Inn, 75; Seabeach, 42; Hustace Villa, 22; Cassidy Place, 35; Hau Tree, 50; lodging houses: Cressaty's, 30.

Activity in the Midst of Tranquility

73 "Everyone went to the beach . . .": *Pacific Commercial Advertiser*, February 2, 1903

75 *Hawaiian Annual for 1911* p. 143 covered the beginnings of the Outrigger Canoe Club. For additional information see Harold H. Yost, *The Outrigger* (Honolulu: 1971).

79 "quite comfortably placed . . ." letter from Winslow to Abbot, November 17, 1908, quoted in Erwin Thompson, *Pacific Ocean Engineers* (Honolulu: U.S. Army Corps of Engineers, 1985) p. 36

80 Histories of St. Augustine's Catholic Church appear in *Star Bulletin*, August 25, 1951 p. 24, and *Honolulu Advertiser*, April 22, 1956, supplement, p. 2.

81 The wreck and destruction of the *Helga* was covered in both the *Pacific Commercial Advertiser* and *Evening Bulletin* from August 11, 1910 through August 20, 1910.

82 "Waikīkī beach yesterday . . . ": *Pacific Commercial Advertiser*, May 12, 1913, p. 9

83 Information on the changing of the garb derives from the following: anonymous confession, *Pacific Commercial Advertiser*, June 9, 1913, p. 9; golden mermaid, *Pacific Commercial Advertiser*, July 14, 1913, p. 9; drama at Waikiki beach, *Star Bulletin*, June 30, 1913, p. 1; Mayor Fern, *Star Bulletin*, July 19, 1913, p. 7 and July 28, 1913, p. 1, and *Pacific Commercial Advertiser*, August 24, 1913, editorial page; "lānai lizards," *Pacific Commercial Advertiser*, June 22, 1918, sec. 2, p. 1; "promenade of nymphs . . .", *Pacific Commercial Advertiser*, June 19, 1918, sec. 2, p. 1: "low necked, sleeveless, legless . . .": *Honolulu Advertiser*, April 23, 1922, editorial; "unless covered suitably . . ." Act 155 of the 1921 Legislature (Chapter 276, Hawaii Revised Statutes).

The Draining of Waikīkī

87 The 1913 conflict over smearing of the beach with rice field flotsam was reported in *Pacific Commercial Advertiser*, February 16, 1913, p. 9.

88 Pinkham, *Hawaii Board of Health Report: The Reclamation of the Waikiki District* (Honolulu, 1906)

For a discussion of the canal and its construction see Barry Seichi Nakamura, "The Story of Waikīkī and the 'Reclamation' Project", unpublished Masters Thesis, University of Hawai'i, 1979.

For information on the controversy over the trees on Kalākaua Avenue see, *Pacific Commercial Advertiser*, March 10, 1912, p. 4.

89 The naming of the canal was covered in the *Honolulu Advertiser*, March 22, 1925, p. 8, and April 5, 1925, p. 12.

90 For more information on Pinkham's appointment see H. Brett Melendy, "The Controversial Appointment of Lucius Eugene Pinkham, Hawaii's First Democratic Governor", *Hawaiian Journal of History*, vol. 17, 1983 pp. 185-208.

91 "often stormy . . . ": *Honolulu Star-Bulletin*, November 2, 1922, editorial. For other newspaper attacks on the governor see: *Pacific Commercial Advertiser*, January 8, 1917, p. 1; January 26, 1917, p. 7; and August 3, 1917, p. 7.

The Grand New Waikīkī

94 The February 1, 1927 *Honolulu Advertiser* contained a special section on the opening of the Royal Hawaiian Hotel.

99 "skyscrapers are . . .": *Honolulu Advertiser*, September 6, 1925

100 "an effort toward the last word . . . ": *Honolulu Advertiser*, October 31, 1927, p. 4. The purchase of the property by Heen Investment Company is covered in *Honolulu Advertiser*, May 23, 1926, p. 10.

103 "personality of the land . . . ": *Star Bulletin*, December 19, 1931, Special Section covers the reopening of the Halekūlani.

"lend age . . ." and "guests of the hotel . . .": *Honolulu Advertiser*, November 11, 1928, Society Section, pp. 15-20 covers the reopening of the Waikīkī Inn

104 "didn't have something to do . . . ": *Honolulu Star-Bulletin*, September 30, 1939, p. 11

Pond's effort to preserve Ka'iulani's banyan is reported in the *Pacific Commercial Advertiser*, May 29, 1919. Under this tree Robert Louis Stevenson met with Princess Ka'iulani in 1889, and at the time of the princess's departure from Hawai'i to attend school in Great Britain, the poet wrote in her album:

> Forth from her land to mine she goes,
> The island maid, the island rose,
> Light of heart and bright of face:
> The daughter of a double race.
> Her islands here, in Southern sun,
> Shall mourn their Kaiulani gone,
> And, I, in her dear banyan shade,
> Look vainly for my little maid.
>
> But our Scots islands far away
> Shall glitter with unwonted day,
> And cast for once their tempests by
> To smile in Kaiulani's eye.
>
> Written in April to Kaiulani in the April of her age; and at Waikiki, within easy walk of Kaiulani's banyan! When she comes to my land and her father's [Scotland], and the rain beats upon the window . . . let her look at this page; it will be like a weed gathered and pressed at home; and she will remember her own Islands, and the shadow of the mighty tree; and she will hear the peacocks screaming in the dusk and the wind blowing in the palm; and she will think of her father sitting there alone . . . RLS

104 "rats, cats, red berries . . . ": *Honolulu Star-Bulletin*, November 11, 1948, p. 10

105 "one of the city's main tourist . . . ": *Honolulu Star-Bulletin*, September 30, 1939, p. 11

106 "the old romantic . . . ": *Honolulu Advertiser*, July 31, 1919, p.1

107 The Carter residence demolition was covered in *Honolulu Advertiser*, June 28, 1960, p. A-8.

Where the Action Was

112 The *Honolulu Advertiser* covered the development and opening of the Aloha Amusement Park. See September 10, 1922, p. 9; September 15, 1922 p.1; and April 9, 1922 p.6 for descriptions of the park. Objections to the park can be found in April 15, 1922 p. 1; April 17, 1922, letters to the editor; April 19, 1922, letters to the editor; and April 21, 1922, letters to the editor.

114 For the opening and closing of Gumps see the *Star Bulletin*, February 19, 1929, p. 11; and *Honolulu Advertiser*, February 24, 1951, p. 1.

117 The opening of Lau Yee Chai was covered in the *Honolulu Advertiser*, December 12, 1929, p.11 and its demolition was covered on March 10, 1966 p. C-10.

120 For the opening of the Waikīkī Theater see *Honolulu Star Bulletin*, August 20, 1936, special supplement.

121 "What was once . . . ": *Honolulu Advertiser* March 6, 1938, Magazine Section, p. 1

122 "mention tradewinds . . . " on the dust jacket of Owens, Harry, *Sweet Leilani, The Story Behind the Song* (Pacific Palisades, California: Hula House, 1970)

123 "a new sweetness of melody . . . " *Honolulu Star-Bulletin*, September 4, 1940, editorial

125 Charlie Chaplin and George Benard Shaw: *Honolulu Advertiser*, February 27, 1936, p. 1

125 Shirley Temple and beach patrol: *Honolulu Advertiser,* August 5, 1935

130 Lālani Village description found in *Paradise of the Pacific,* April 1934, pp.11-14; September 1936, p. 15+; and *Star Bulletin,* September 21, 1963 p. 3. Reference to the "Hawaiian renaissance", appeared in *The Hawaiian Annual for 1932,* p. 40.

Waikīkī Takes Off: Tourism in the 1950s

135 The opening of the Rosalei appeared in *Star Bulletin,* March 8, 1955, p. 12

136 Information on the Princess Ka'iulani Hotel may be found in *Honolulu Advertiser,* June 11, 1955, Special Supplement, and *Paradise of the Pacific,* July 1955, pp. 26-31+.

140 Time has proven the "wild" figure of 750 rooms to be rather conservative. By 1962 the construction of the Reef Tower and its addition expanded the Reef Hotel's capacity to 883 rooms. In 1986 the Hilton Hawaiian Village boasted 2,612 rooms; the Sheraton Waikīkī 1,852; the Hawaiian Regent 1,346; the Hyatt Regency 1,234; the Princess Ka'iulani 1,156; the Pacific Beach 850; and the 'Ilikai 801.

140 "Anything can happen . . . ": *Honolulu Advertiser,* October 23, 1955, supplement, p. 2

141 "I have had implicit . . . ": *Honolulu Advertiser,* June 13, 1954, p. C-3

144 The opening of the Hawaiian Village was covered in *Honolulu Advertiser,* September 18, 1955, Section E.

Waikīkī Today

149 "17,000 residents in the district": This number is based on the 1980 Federal Census. Inventories taken by the Waikīkī Improvement Association and the Waikīkī Neighborhood Board indicate that these figures may be low by at least 5,000 people.

"(81%) were born outside Hawai'i": 1980 Federal Census figures. In comparison, 55% of the people dwelling in Honolulu inhaled Island air in their first breath of life.

"72% of them resided in their present dwelling for less than five years.": According to 1980 Federal

Census figures 48% of Honolulu's population could claim such permanency. Considering even more long term stability, only 1.46% of the housing units in Waikīkī, a total of 43, were occupied in 1980 by the same persons who lived there at the time of Statehood (1959), but throughout the state this was true for 17.87% of the residential units. A further indication of the temporary character of Waikīkī's residential base lay in the fact that 70% of Waikīkī's housing units were renter-occupied in 1980, as compared with 48% throughout the Islands.

149 "98% of the district's housing": 1980 Federal Census figures. In contrast, throughout the state structures with five or more units only accounted for 40% of the residential units, while single family dwellings constituted 47% of the Islands' housing stock. However, downtown Honolulu housing unit figures are comparable to those of Waikīkī. Census figures also indicate that the inhabitants of Waikīkī not only are less connected to the land, but also their personal relationships are in greater flux. Only 37% of the people living in the district are married, as compared to 57% of the state's population. Oddly enough, the percentage of single (i.e. never married) people in the area is consistent with Hawai'i's overall figures (33% and 32%, respectively). However, where only 6% of the state's populace are divorced, 17% of Waikīkī's residents have dissolved their marriages. Another 3% of the district's denizens are separated from their spouses, while only 1% of Hawai'i's people find themselves in such a situation.

159 "why Hawai'i is a better . . . ": *Paradise of the Pacific,* March 1962, "The Million Dollar Image", pp. 6-7

160 For the demolition of the Biltmore see *Star Bulletin,* May 28, 1974, p. B-1, and *Honolulu Advertiser,* May 29, 1974, p. A-3.

164 "a bright episode . . . ": for these descriptions see *Honolulu Advertiser,* September 21, 1961 p. A1 c. 6, and *Honolulu Advertiser* October 23, 1955, supplement, p. 2

168 Information on the Rainbow Bazaar may be found in *Star Bulletin,* June 1, 1970, p. A-2; and *Honolulu Advertiser,* February 2, 1972, A-13

170 Lois Taylor quotation in the *Honolulu Star Bulletin,* July 15, 1971, p. E1

174 For a discussion of the erosion problem and a good general description of the beach at Waikīkī prior to the Corps of Engineers activities, see "Hawaii's Skin Game", in *The Honolulu Times,* May 30, 1931, p.5, which noted, "There is a beach, of a sort, but it's not

the beach we advertise, not the beach tourists come thousands of miles to enjoy.

"The water is there, the most soothing, entrancing water in the world. But, for the most part, it laps, not on smooth, clean sand, but on ugly concrete walls.

"And what little sand there is—only a narrow strip between selfish walls—is littered with debris, such as cigarette butts, orange and banana peels, smelly seaweed, chunks of coral, paunchy fat men and 'kept' beach boys."

176 "conglomerate of look-alike . . . ": *Star Bulletin,* June 28, 1972, editorial page. For other information on King's Alley, see *Honolulu Advertiser,* November 26, 1971, p. B4.

Waikīkī Tomorrow

214 *Popular Mechanics* news item quoted in *Pacific Commercial Advertiser,* June 30, 1912, p. 11

215 "Whatever is done . . . ," Mumford, Lewis, *A Memorandum Report on Park and City Planning—Whither Honolulu?* (Honolulu: 1938), p. 66

"the chain of parks . . . ": *ibid,* p. 27

Mumford's makeshift improvements warning appears in *ibid,* pp. 48-49.

218 "Hawaiian type Coney Island . . . ": *Honolulu Advertiser,* August 21, 1938, p. 14

"unnecessary and expensive . . . ": *Honolulu Advertiser,* August 26, 1938, p. 1

"demnition bowwows . . . ": *Honolulu Star-Bulletin,* December 31, 1938, p. 6

"find much of it is . . . ": *Honolulu Star-Bulletin,* December 22, 1938, p. 8

219 "67 pages of . . . ": *Honolulu Star-Bulletin,* December 29, 1938, p. 1

"Mr. Mumford has some . . . ": *Honolulu Advertiser,* January 8, 1938, editorial

"no attention was paid . . . ": *Honolulu Advertiser,* November 23, 1947, editorial

220 "reorient the people . . . ": *Waikīkī 2000, A Proposal to Revitalize Waikīkī,* (Honolulu: 1981), p. 2

221 "innovation to conceive . . . ": Mumford, p. 67

"Waikīkī shortcut . . . ," *ibid,* p 53

No other city . . . ," *ibid,* p. 7

Photographic Credits

The Seat of Power

pp. 2-3: Dampier print, Bishop Museum; p. 4: Diamond Head, Hawai'i State Archives; Helumoa grove, Bishop Museum; p. 5: wizard stones, Franzen Photography; p. 6: map, Hawai'i State Survey Division, Department of Accounting and General Services; p. 7: Burgess print, Hawai'i State Archives

Victorian Waikīkī — The Playground of Royalty

p. 8: Queen Lili'uokalani cottage, Hawai'i State Archives; p. 9: Queen Emma cottage, Bishop Museum; p. 10: Bishop cottage, Hawai'i State Archives; pp. 10-11: Kamehameha V cottage, Hawai'i Mission Children's Society; p. 11: King Kalākaua and Queen Kapi'olani cottage Hawai'i State Archives; pp. 12-13: Archibald Cleghorn and 'Āinahau, all photos, Hawai'i State Archives; p. 15: map, Hawai'i State Survey Division, Department of Accounting and General Services; p. 16-17: croquet players, and Duke of Edinburgh, Hawai'i State Archives; p. 18: Stevenson and Hoffnung lū'au, Hawai'i State Archives; p. 19: Lili'uokalani's pier, Bishop Museum

From Mosquitoes to Mansions

pp. 20-21: McInerny cottage, Bishop Museum; p. 22: Mitchells', Bishop Museum; pp. 22-23: Waikīkī Road and Waikīkī Beach, Hawai'i State Archives; p. 24: Cordelia, Mrs. Joseph Gilman,; pp. 24-25: Hawaiian fishermen, Hawaiian Historical Society; p. 25: Bertelmann cottage, Hawai'i State Archives; and bicyclist, Bishop Museum; p. 26: McInerny and Dole cottages, Bishop Museum; p. 27: Hustace residence, Bishop Museum; p. 28: Campbell residence, Gaylord Wilcox; p. 29: Irwin residence, Bishop Museum; pp. 30-31: Steiner residence, front and interior, Keith Steiner; ocean view Army Corps of Engineers; pp. 32-35: Castle residence, Bishop Museum; p. 36: Deering residence, Hawai'i State Archives; pp. 37-39: Prince Kūhiō residence, Bishop Museum; pp. 40-41: Dillingham and La Pietra, Hawai'i State Archives; polo team, Bishop Museum

Kapi'olani Park

pp. 42-43: Kapi'olani Park and bridge, Hawai'i State Archives; Camp McKinley, US Army Museum; pp. 44-45: Makee Island, all photographs from Hawai'i State Archives; p. 46 park road, Bishop Museum; aquarium, Hawai'i State Archives; p. 47: Makee Island bandstand, Hawaiian Historical Society; lava rock bandstand, Bishop Museum; pp. 48-49: Daisy the elephant, all photos Bishop Museum except Ben Hollinger, City and County of Honolulu; p. 50: aerial view of natatorium, Army Corps of Engineers; p. 51: Phoenix Fountain, Hawaiian Historical Society

Bathhouses and Hostelries

p. 52: Long Branch on beach, Hawaiian Historical Society; p. 53: toboggan, Bishop Museum; man on beach, Hawai'i State Archives; p. 54: Waikīkī Villa, Hawai'i State Archives; p. 55: night view, Bishop Museum; p. 56: Park Beach Hotel, Hawai'i State Archives; p. 57: Sans Souci, Bishop Museum; Sans Souci lānai, Hawai'i State Archives; p. 58: roof garden, *Paradise of the Pacific*; Moana Hotel, Hawai'i State Archives; p. 59: Moana and Long Branch Baths, Peter Thacker; pp. 60-61: Moana Hotel, all photographs Hawai'i State Archives, except view from the pier, Hawaiian Historical Society; pp. 62-63: Seaside Hotel and Jack London, all photographs Hawai'i State Archives; p. 64: Alice Roosevelt, Hawai'i State Archives; p. 65: Longworth cottage and teatime, Bishop Museum; p. 67: Jack London, Hawai'i State Archives, pp. 66-67: both photos of Colonel G. W. Macfarlane, Hawai'i State Archives; all others, Mrs. Muriel Flanders; p. 68: Waikīkī Inn advertisement, Polk's City Directory; p. 69: Cressaty's, Bishop Museum; Gilman residence, Mrs. Joseph Gilman; and Lewers residence, *Pan-Pacific Magazine*; p. 70: Snapshot and Hau Tree lānai, Bishop Museum; p. 71: 'Āinahau, Hawai'i State Archives

Activity in the Midst of Tranquility

pp. 72-73: Kalākaua Avenue and laying the cable, Bishop Museum; p. 74: 1907 public baths, City and County of Honolulu; 1931 public baths, Bishop Museum; pp. 75-77: all Outrigger Canoe Club, Hawai'i State Archives; except canoe shed, Hawaiian Mission Children's Society; pp. 78-79: all Fort DeRussy, U.S. Army Museum; p. 79: map, Hawai'i State Survey Division, Department of Accounting and General Services; p. 80: St. Augustine's Church, Catholic Archives of the Diocese of Honolulu; p. 81: wreck of the *Helga*, Mrs. Joseph Gilman; p. 82 surfer, Hawaiian Historical Society; beach scene, Hawai'i State Archives; p. 83: Gertrude McQueen, Bishop Museum

The Draining of Waikīkī

p. 84: 'Āinahau gardens, Hawai'i State Archives; p. 85: looking upstream, Hawaiian Mission Children's Society; p. 86: Waikīkī Road, Hawaiian Historical Society; fishponds, Bishop Museum; p. 87: duck pond, Hawaiian Historical Society; p. 88: dredge at Kalākaua avenue, Hawai'i State Archives; rear of dredge, Bishop Museum; p. 89: Jennie Wilson, Hawai'i State Archives; p. 90: Pinkham, Hawai'i State Archives; p. 91: view from Moana, *Paradise of the Pacific*; aerial photograph, Army Corps of Engineers; p. 92: fishing, Hawai'i State Archives; p. 93: aerial: Hawai'i State Archives

The Grand New Waikīkī

pp. 94-99: Royal Hawaiian views, Hawai'i State Archives; except aerial, Army Corps of Engineers; p. 100: Niumalu Hotel, Bishop Museum; p. 101: Niumalu Hotel, Hawai'i State Archives; p. 102: Waikīkī Inn from Kalākaua Avenue, Bishop Museum, and Halekūlani, Hawai'i State Archives; p. 103: advertisement, *Honolulu Advertiser*; p. 104-105: Percy Pond and Ka'iulani's Banyan, Hawai'i State Archives; Lili'uokalani Avenue, Bishop Museum; p. 106: advertisement, *Honolulu Advertiser*; p. 107: Carter residence, Mrs. Frank Midkiff; Inn Bungalows, Henry Inn; aerial, Army Corps of Engineers

Where the Action Was

p. 108 Aloha Amusement Park, Hawai'i State Archives; p. 109: Aloha Amusement Park, Bishop Museum; pp. 110-111: Fairground fireworks, Bishop Museum; p. 112: Beach Barber Shop, and Banzai Cleaners, Mrs. H. Kono; p. 113: Aoki Store, Harold Aoki; p. 114: Gumps, Hawai'i State Archives; advertisement, *Honolulu Advertiser*; p. 115: Elmer Lee and Helen Kimball, *Honolulu Advertiser*; p. 116: Lili's Lei Stand, Lilinoe Sniffen; Richards taxi, Mervin Richards; p. 117: Lau Yee Chai exterior, Lau Yee Chai; advertisement, *Honolulu Advertiser*; p. 118: Kau Kau Korner, Bishop Museum; KDI, Kenton Tom; p. 119: KC Drive-In, Green Lantern, Hawai'i State Archives; p. 120: exterior, Consolidated Amusement; interior, DeSoto Brown; p. 121: Franzen Photography; except aerial, Army Corps of Engineers; pp. 122-123: Harry Owens, Hawai'i State Archives; Johnny Noble Orchestra, Charlie Lambert; pp. 124-129: famous and near-famous, Hawai'i State Archives; pp. 130-131: all Lālani Village, Bishop Museum; except Vicki Baum, Hawai'i State Archives

Wartime Waikīkī

pp. 132-133: Joe DiMaggio and barbed wire beach, Hawai'i State Archives

Waikīkī Takes Off: Tourism in the 1950s

pp. 134-137: view from Rosalei Apartments, Rosalei Apartments, and Princess Ka'iulani, by Robert Wenkam, courtesy Salbosa Photography; p. 138: view from Kūhiō Avenue, historic, Army Corps of Engineers, and contemporary, Franzen Photography; p. 139: view from Kalākaua Avenue, Ron Lee; view of Lewers Street, Army Corps of Engineers; pp. 140-141: Roy Kelley, Roy Kelley; pp. 142-145: McInerney Store, Bishop Bank, Waikikian and Hawaiian Village, by Robert Wenkam, courtesy Salbosa Photography

Waikīkī Today

All photographs Franzen Photography except, p. 155, sand castle, Liz Squires, and p. 160, demolition of the Waikīkī Biltmore, *Honolulu Advertiser*

Waikīkī Tomorrow

p. 210: 'Tomorrow', painting by Ashley Bickerton, courtesy of Jack Schweigert; p. 212: 1920s future vision, *Honolulu Advertiser*; p. 213: 1940s future vision, Hawaiian Electric; p. 214: 1960s future vision, *Paradise of the Pacific*; p. 215: reef hotel, *Honolulu Advertiser*; p. 216: advertisement, *Honolulu Advertiser*; p. 217: Royal Hawaiian Shopping Center proposal, Charles R. Sutton & Associates; pp. 218-219: Mumford, *Time*; Ala Wai park area, Franzen Photography; pp. 220-221: Group Seventy proposal, Lisa Pongrace from originals by Ron Lee

Index